Physical Charact
Welsh Spring

(from the American Kennel Club breed standard)

Topline: Level.

Tail: Is an extension of the topline. The tail is generally docked.

Hindquarters: Strong, muscular and well boned, but not coarse. The angulation of the pelvis and femur corresponds to that of the shoulder and upper arm. Bend of stifle is moderate. The bones from the hocks to the pads are short with a well angulated hock joint. When viewed from the side or rear they are perpendicular to the ground.

Coat: Naturally straight, flat and soft to the touch, never wiry or wavy. It is sufficiently dense to be waterproof, thornproof and weatherproof.

Size: A dog is ideally 18–19 inches in height at the withers and a bitch is 17–18 inches at the withers.

Color: Rich red and white only.

Welsh Springer Spaniel

By Haja van Wessem

Contents

Training Your Welsh Springer Spaniel 94

Begin with the basics of training the puppy and adult dog. Learn the principles of house-training the Welshie, including the use of crates and basic scent instincts. Get started by introducing the pup to his collar and leash and progress to the basic commands. Find out about obedience classes, field training and other activities.

Healthcare of Your Welsh Springer Spaniel 121

By Lowell Ackerman DVM, DACVD
Become your dog's healthcare advocate and a well-educated canine keeper. Select a skilled and able veterinarian. Discuss pet insurance, vaccinations and infectious diseases, the neuter/spay decision and a sensible, effective plan for parasite control, including fleas, ticks and worms.

Showing Your Welsh Springer Spaniel 144

Step into the center ring and find out about the world of showing pure-bred dogs. Here's how to get started in AKC shows, how they are organized and what's required for your dog to become a champion. Also take a leap into the realms of obedience trials, agility trials, field trials, hunting tests and more.

KENNEL CLUB BOOKS® WELSH SPRINGER SPANIEL
ISBN: 1-59378-269-1

Copyright © 2007 • Kennel Club Books, LLC • 308 Main Street, Allenhurst, NJ 07711 USA
Cover Design Patented: US 6,435,559 B2 • Printed in South Korea

Library of Congress Cataloging-in-Publication Data
Van Wessem, Haja.
    Welsh springer spaniel / by Haja van Wessem.
        p. cm.
1. Welsh springer spaniel. I. Title.
SF429.W37V36 2007
636.752'4—dc22
                                    2006016289

10 9 8 7 6 5 4 3 2 1

Photography by Isabelle Français
with additional photographs by:

Ashbey Photography, Adrienne Bancker, Norvia Behling, Paulette Braun, Carolina Biological Supply, David Dalton, Tara Darling, Joan Hamaguchi, Beth Holmes, Helga Horsten, Ria Hörter, Carol Ann Johnson, Gundrun Johnson, Bill Jonas, Dr. Dennis Kunkel, Keith Lyle, Tam C. Nguyen, Marinus Nijhoff, Colleen M. O'Keefe, Perry Phillips, Phototake, Mrs. J. A. R. Revill, Jean Claude Revy, Susan Riese, J. Schotte-Slootweg, Stonham Photography, Paul Tapar, Tien Tran, Alice van Kempen and Haja van Wessem.

Illustrations by Angela Begg and Patricia Peters.

The publisher wishes to thank all of the owners whose dogs are illustrated in this book, including Adrienne Bancker, Meghen Riese Bassel, Carl & Fran Bloom, Linda S. Brennan, Nora Carlton, Connie Christie, Laurie Dietz, Cindy Ford, Mike & Anne Gilliam, Joan Hamaguchi, Hammalgårdens kennel, Beth Holmes, Harry Holmes, Sandra N. Holmes, Ria Hörter, David & Lisa Hubler, Janet & Tom Ing, George & Sandy Lear, Anne Legare, Karen Lyle, Tom & Susan Neal, Marinus Nijhoff, Susan Riese, Sandra & Richard Rohrbacher, Peggy Ruble, Dennis & Jody Stegall, Tiny van Gent-Slootweg, Shelley Traylor, Jürgen Wallat, Haja van Wessem, Chris Wheeler, Mr. S. & Mrs. H. Williams and Sue Willingham.

Special thanks to Joan Hamaguchi and Beth Holmes.

WELSH SPRINGER SPANIEL

EARLY SPANIEL HISTORY

Legend has it that there were springer spaniels as far back as the 16th century. True or not, a fact is that the whole group of spaniels, to which the Welsh Springer Spaniel belongs, can be considered among the oldest dogs known to man. It is very likely that the spaniel got his name from the country surrounding the Mediterranean where he lived, namely Spain. According to other sources, he might have got his name from the word *España* or from the several spaniel-like breeds in France that are called *épagneuls*. The name "spaniel" might also have been derived from the French *s'éspargner*, which means "to crouch."

Spaniels also traveled to Wales, where they were the treasured dogs of King Hywel Dda (Howell the Good). The king's love for his spaniels went as far as giving them a special mention in one of the country's laws in AD 948: for the price of one spaniel, one could buy a number of goats, women, slaves or geese! However, in recent years the authenticity of this document has been questioned.

The first mention of a spaniel in English literature comes as early as Geoffrey Chaucer (1340–1400). In *The Canterbury Tales*, Chaucer refers to the spaniel several times (e.g., "for as a spaynel she wol on him lepe"), which proves that the spaniel was known in England 600 years ago.

Gaston de Foix, who died in 1391, mentions the spaniel in his work *Miroir de Phoebus* or, as it is also known, *Livre de Chasse*. A feudal baron who lived in France near the Spanish border, de Foix was convinced that Spain was the country of origin of the spaniel. "Another kind of hound there is, that be called hounds for the hawk, and spaniels, for their kind cometh from Spain, notwithstanding that there are many in other countries. And such hounds have many good customs and evil. Also a fair hound for the hawk should have a great head, a great body, and be of fair hue, white or tawny (i.e., pied, speckled or mottled) for they be fairest and of such hue they be commonly the best. They go before their master, running and wagging their tail, and raise or start fowl and wild beasts. But their right craft is of the partridge and of the quail. They can also be taught to take partridge and quail with the net and they love to swim."

Another early reference to "Spanyellys" occurs in the *Boke of St. Albans* (1486), also named the *Book of Field Sports*, written by Dame Juliana Berners, prioress of Sopwell Nunnery, Hertfordshire. It is obviously a school book and it is assumed that the book was written for the use of the royal princes, to teach them to read and make them acquainted with the names of the animals and phrases used in venery and field sports. In the book there is frequent mention of spaniels in the royal household. Thus we read that "Robin, the King's Majesty's Spaniel Keeper" was paid a certain sum for "hair cloth to rub the Spaniels with."

THE FIRST SPRINGERS
We find the first mention of springer spaniels and in particular red and white spaniels in the book *Treatise of Englishe Dogges* (1570) by the famed dog scholar Dr. Caius (pseudonym for John

A member of the spaniel family, which are some of the oldest dogs known to man, the Welsh Springer Spaniel is a distinguished gundog who is as striking as he is talented.

Three Welsh Springers owned by Mr. J. S. Jones, photographed at their Crufts debut in 1934.

Keyes). Dr. Caius described the way the dogs were taught to let themselves be caught under the net, and he classified all sporting dogs under two headings: *Venatici*, used for the purpose of hunting beasts, and *Auscupatorii*, used for the hunting of fowl. He subdivided this latter group into land spaniels and spaniels "which findeth game on the water." He named this group *Hispaniolus*. He also was of the opinion that these dogs originated in Spain. He refers to "the spanniells whose skynnes are white, and if they are marcked with any spottes, they are commonly red."

In the days of Henry VIII, the many royal banquets required great amounts of food, particularly game. Game such as partridge, quail, pheasant, rabbit and hare were caught in snares but because of the never-ending demand, a more speedy method of catching

the game was needed. This method was found in "netting." Spaniels were used to drive the birds toward the fowlers, who stood ready with their extended nets. Dog and bird were caught under the net. The spaniels that were used for this kind of work were called "sitting" or "setting" spaniels, and they are the ancestors of our modern setters.

With the advent of reliable guns, netting disappeared and game was caught by shooting. The setting spaniels were used to find the game and point it, and the springing spaniel flushed the game from the cover so that it could be shot.

In the *Sportsman's Cabinet*, written by Nicolas Cox and published in 1803, we find this description of the spaniel: "The true-bred, English-bred Springer Spaniel differs but little in figure from the Setter, except in size varying only a small degree, if any, from a red, yellow or liver color and white, which seems to be the invariable external standard of this breed. They are nearly two-fifths less in height and strength than the Setter, delicately formed, ears long, soft and pliable, coat waving and silky, eyes and nose red or black, the tail bushy and pendulous, always in motion when actively employed." Other indirect evidence of the existence of red and white dogs can be found in the 18th century work *A Treatise on Field Diversions* by the Reverend B. Symonds of Kelsale, Suffolk. He mentions two coat colors, black tanned and orange or lemon and white, and two types, short- and long-waved coats.

In the 1800s, the term "springing spaniel" was gaining ground as a description not of a particular variety but of the group of gundogs that sprang their game. All land spaniels came under this heading, and the varieties we now know as the Clumber, Welsh Springer, English Springer, Field, Cocker and Sussex Spaniel were all springing spaniels.

Although it appears that the red and white spaniels were well distributed throughout Britain at one time, during the 18th and 19th centuries they were confined mainly to the Neath Valley in South Wales. Evidence thereof is found in the book *Dogs in Britain* by the late Clifford Hubbard, renowned authority on dogs. He wrote, "The spaniels of Wales were almost all red and white, and it is certain that the Welsh Springer Spaniel is descended from a type which was common to Wales and seldom found elsewhere till comparatively recent years."

Mr. A. T. Williams, who was to play such an important part in the founding of the breed, told of his family using Welsh Spaniels for sporting purposes. They were very uniform in type but varying in color. The flesh-colored nose was considered to be more correct than the black, whereas today the standard requires nostrils to be black or brown and the coat rich red and white only. Still, flesh-colored noses and lighter shades of red are sometimes seen.

The spaniel situation was a mixed bag, with offspring of English Springers being registered as Field Spaniels or Welsh Spaniels according to their size and/or color, and Cockers and Field Spaniels being born in the same litters, registered according to their weight.

Crossbreeding had always occurred in working circles, but links between the newly separated breeds of spaniel were open, and crossbreeding was done regularly. The real Welsh Springer history probably begins with Corrin, who was born in 1893 and who competed success-

Pat of Merrymount was a very prolific and successful sire of many fine Welsh Springers. He was owned by the Reverend D. Stewart, who was one of the great promoters of the breed.

Scott Langley, British canine artist, made this sketch titled *Welsh Springer Spaniels* in 1931.

fully in the show ring with all other kinds of sporting spaniels. He was bred by Colonel Blandy-Jenkins of Llanharan and was owned by Mr. A. T. Williams (Gerwn). Although Corrin himself was registered as a Welsh Cocker, born of two red and white parents, his offspring were variously registered. Bred to Mena of Gerwn, he produced Rover of Gerwn, probably Mr. Williams's best Welsh Springer and, after the breed had been recognized as a separate variety, the first Welsh Springer Spaniel champion. Rover, bred to Belle of Gerwn, produced Duke of Gerwn, who was black and white, and Roverson of Gerwn, who was liver and white. Both of them can be found in the pedigrees of American and Canadian field-trial English Springers.

In 1902 it was Mr. Williams who, together with a group of

Welsh gentlemen that included Colonel Blandy-Jenkins, offered the evidence to The Kennel Club of England that the Welsh Springer Spaniel was a separate breed, different from the English Springer Spaniel. Mr. Williams could trace his family's kennel back to the end of the 18th century, and the other gentlemen could affirm that this breed of dog had been kept for many years in their families' kennels. Mr. Williams's plea was successful, and the Welsh Springer Spaniel was recognized as a separate variety by The Kennel Club in 1902.

Soon after recognition, the Welsh Spaniel Club was founded. The first secretary was Mrs. H. D. Greene. Her Longmynd prefix still lives on in the most famous breed picture by Maud Earl in 1906, which depicts two of her champions, Eng. Ch. Longmynd Myfanwy and Eng. Ch. Longmynd Megan.

Although the breed did fairly well, being popular as a working dog, breed activities came to a halt in 1914 when World War I broke out. After the war it was Colonel Downes-Powell who revived the activities and formed a new club, the Welsh Springer Spaniel Club.

The club set out to safeguard the dual-purpose (show and field) ideal as much as possible, and emphasis was placed on working qualities. The number of Welsh Springers registered annually in the years between the two World Wars was around 100, but there might well have been many more, living as pets or working dogs, that were not registered. At the shows, between 10 and 20 Welsh were entered, increasing to 30 to 40 just before World War II. The center of activity was still based in Wales.

Outstanding dogs of this period were F. Morris's Eng. Ch. Barglam Bang, Colonel Downes-Powell's Eng. Ch. Marksman O'Matherne and Eng. Ch. Musketeer O'Matherne and Mr. A. J. Dyke's Ch. Marglam Marquis. It must be remembered that in order to become a champion in those

Eng. Ch. Musketeer O' Matherne was bred in July 1932 by Capt. J. Gage-Williams.

days, a dog had to win both on the bench and in the field.

Just before World War II, three new breeders, notably Harold Newman (Pencelli), Cliff Payne (Tregwillym) and Hal Leopard (Rushbrooke), began their programs and would have, as history proves, a tremendous influence on the breed.

Mr. Leopard's bitch Goitre Lass had nine litters, and her name can be seen in quite a few pedigrees. According to Mr. Leopard, who thought Goitre Lass came from a Cocker or English Springer mating, she was the origin of the dark-nosed strain of Welsh Springer. For a long time, pink noses and hazel eyes as well as dark noses and dark eyes were seen, and it is believed that Goitre Lass progeny started this fashion for dark noses, which is the preferred color nowadays.

World War II was not as damaging to the breed as World War I, as there were more dogs, with the majority of them being in

ON POSTAGE STAMPS

The Welsh Springer Spaniel is featured on stamps in many countries, but the best one is probably the one issued by the General Post Office in Great Britain. It is a 10 ½-pence stamp, featuring a rendering of the *Tarfgi Cymreig* (the breed's Welsh name) by the artist Peter Barrett.

South Wales, which was less threatened by the war than London and the Midlands.

Colonel Downes-Powell ("the Colonel") more or less kept the breed club going. It turned out to be an extremely wise move when he asked Harold Newman officially to continue the breed, a nomination of which Harold was very proud. Harold, who already had had some success in the 1930s with Barmaid and Eng. Sh. Ch. Dere Mhlaen, concentrated purely on the show ring, but breeders such as Marjorie Mayall and A. J. Dyke remained dual-purpose enthusiasts and safeguarded the working abilities of the breed.

In the 1950s the Tregwillym kennels of Cliff Payne started to dominate the ring. Token of Tregwillym, Top Score of Tregwillym, Statesman of Tregwillym and Trigger of Tregwillym became champions. Token of Tregwillym was top dog in 1956 and again in 1957 when he tied with Top Score of Tregwillym.

By that time The Kennel Club had decided to introduce the titles of Show Champion for a dog that had won three Challenge Certificates (CCs, also called "tickets"), Champion for the dog that had won three CCs and had also qualified in the field and Dual Champion for a dog that had obtained the titles of Show Champion and Field Trial Champion.

Mr. and Mrs. Morgan sold their Brancourt kennel to Mr. T. Hubert Arthur, who already was a noted Cocker breeder, and his Eng. Sh. Ch. Brancourt Belinda was top bitch in 1958, 1959 and 1960. One of the first Welsh Springers to win Group honors was Ann West's Eng. Sh. Ch. Deri Darrell of Linkhill (by Eng. Ch.

A "STARTER"

Another name for the Welsh Springer is "starter" which is derived from "to start," meaning to spring the game. Its Welsh equivalent, *tarfgi*, is more commonly used in Wales than the term "Springer."

increasingly turned to the shows. The field-trial enthusiasts eventually decided to move away to a separate field-trial club, established by Mr. Leopard.

Throughout this period the breed started to grow in numbers. The breed's popularity could be seen at the shows, as there were more CCs to offer and the class sizes and total show entries increased, making competition quite keen. The '70s and '80s were

Eng. Sh. Ch. Plattburn Pinetree, bred and owned by Mr. Ken Burgess, pictured here in 1977.

Statesman of Tregwillym), who was Reserve in the Gundog Group at Crufts three times and won an all-breed Best in Show in 1964. Eng. Sh. Ch. Golden Tint of Tregwillym (by Sportsman of Tregwillym) started winning her tickets in 1965 and ended up as a record breaker with 33 CCs.

In 1967 the Plattburn kennels started to attract attention. The breeder, Ken Burgess, finished Paramount and Penny, and Progressor became top dog in 1971. Burgess exported many quality dogs to countries such as the Netherlands and Australia and also to Scandinavia where they formed, together with Dalati exports, the basis for the "modern type" of the breed.

The 1960s and '70s were good years for the breed. Clever breeders managed to keep the type and quality intact. Though the Welsh Springer Club continued to encourage both work and show, the emphasis among the members

A WORK OF ART

In 1999, the Crufts catalog, schedules and posters, all carried a reproduction of a painting of two Welsh Springer Spaniels by Maud Earl (1864–1943), namely Eng. Ch. Longmynd Myfanwy and Eng. Ch. Longmynd Megan. Both were born in 1904, bred and owned by Mrs. H. D. Greene, and were big winners in their day. The original painting is in the possession of England's Kennel Club and on display in its London office.

Eng. Sh. Ch. Dalati Del, bred and owned by Mr. and Mrs. N. Hunton-Morgans, winning at Crufts in 1973.

Eng. Sh. Ch. Progress of Pencelli, bred and owned by Harold Newman in the mid-1970s.

in 1972 and 1973 (in a tie with Tregwillym Golden Gem); and Contessa of Tregwillym, who won Best in Show at the Welsh Kennel Club show in 1975.

It was definitely a loss for the Welsh Springer fraternity when in 1980, at the age of only 69, after 51 years of activity as a breeder and exhibitor, Harold Newman passed away.

Cliff Payne's influence on the breed has been widespread. He

truly golden years for the Welsh Springer Spaniel with an abundance of quality and type and names that cannot be forgotten. Harold Newman, Cliff Payne, Noel and Dodo Hunton-Morgans (Dalati), Maggie Mullins (Athelwood) and Gordon Pattinson (Tidemarsh) all came into the ring with unforgettable dogs: Plattburn Perchance, Progressor, Pinetree and Peewit (who later went to the Netherlands); Dalati Del, top bitch

was a defender of the working qualities of the breed, a shooting enthusiast and a leader and adviser for other breeders. Over the years he won over 150 CCs with his dogs, 30 of them won by Eng. Sh. Ch. Contessa of Tregwillym alone. Dogs of his breeding became the foundation stock for kennels such as Athelwood, Brent, Bramblebank, Hillpark, Krackton, Tidemarsh and Wainfelin. His exports such as Eng. Sh. Ch. Trigger of

Mr. Harold Newman (Pencelli) and Mr. Cliff Payne (Tregwillym) in the early 1970s.

and Eng. Sh. Ch. Dalati Sarian deserve special mention. Sioni himself won 18 CCs and became a top producer in the breed with 23 English Show Champion offspring. He died in 1996 at the age of 14. Sarian, by Tregwillym Royal Mint, was a Group winner at Crufts and won a total of 37 CCs.

Eng. Sh. Ch. Wainfelin Barley Mo, also by Tregwillym Royal Mint, bred and owned by Mansel and Avril Young, was for a long time the breed record holder with 41 CCs until Eng. Sh. Ch. Russethill Royal Salute over Nyliram, by Eng. Sh. Ch. Dalati Sioni, bred by Doreen Gately and owned by Tom Graham, came along. "Harvey" was top Welsh Springer in 1992, 1993 and 1994.

Eng. Sh. Ch. Dalati Sarian winning at the 1987 championship show.

Eng. Sh. Ch. Wainfelin Barley Mo, winner of 41 CCs.

Tregwillym to the US, Eng. Sh. Ch. Nobleman of Tregwillym to Finland and Eng. Sh. Ch. Tregwillym Golden Gem to New Zealand not only were world famous but also became the foundation stock for the breed in those countries.

A special mention must be made of the Dalati Welsh Springers of Noel and Dodo Hunton-Morgans. They started in the 1960s and over the years produced many champions, of whom Eng. Ch. Dalati Del, tied for top bitch in 1972 and 1973 (with Eng. Sh. Ch. Tregwillym Golden Gem), Eng. Sh. Ch. Dalati Sioni

The author, judging UK breed record-holder Eng. Sh. Ch. Russethill Royal Salute over Nyliram.

Julita (Julie Revill), Highclare (Gill Tully) and Ferndel (John Thirlwell). Thirlwell's first champion was Dalati Gwent, but he has bred an impressive number of champions, of whom Eng. Sh. Ch. Ferndel Stroller became famous as a stud dog and Eng. Sh. Ch. Ferndel Cecilia was probably the one who gained her title the quickest. She needed just three shows to win three CCs and ended up as top Welsh Springer in 1999. In 1996 and 1998 he successfully showed Eng. Sh. Ch. Dalville Dancing Water (by Ferndel Dancing Brave), a bitch he co-owned with her breeder, Ruth Dalrymple. She was Best in Show at the Ladies Kennel Club show in 1997.

With a total of 58 CCs, he is still the UK breed record holder.

Nowadays there are many successful kennels in the UK such as Cwrt Afon (Len and Kate Morgan), Northey (Christine McDonald), Taimere (Graham and Lesley Tain), Weslave (John and Joy Hartley), Parkmist (Trudy and Bill Short), Kazval (Frank Whyte),

Eng. Sh. Ch. Ferndel Cecilia was top bitch and top Welsh in

Eng. Sh. Ch. Highclare Rorkes Drift (left) and Eng. Sh. Ch. Dalville Dancing Water, handled by breeder Ruth Dalrymple.

1999; Eng. Sh. Ch. Hillpark Music
of the Night, bred by Anne Walton,
was top dog in 1999. Jean Taylor's
Eng. Sh. Ch. Cleavehill Brynberrys
was the top Welshie in 2001. She
won Group Two at Crufts and was
Best in Show at the Darlington
Championship Show.

Ferndel dogs were again at the
top in 2002, 2003 and 2004. Eng.
Sh. Ch. Ferndel Cecilia was Best
of Breed at Crufts in 2002. Her
son, Eng. Sh. Ch. Ferndel
Copywrite, was not only top
Welsh Springer but also top
gundog in 2003. He was Best of
Breed at Crufts in 2003 and 2004,
earning Group placements both
years as well. In 2004 the top
Welshie was another son of
Cecilia, Eng. Sh. Ch. Ferndel
Maverick. Although in 2005 Eng.
Sh. Ch. Ferndel Parody (out of
Cecilia as well) was top Welsh
Springer, it was Eng. Sh. Ch.
Ferndel Maverick who won both
Best of Breed and the Gundog
Group. It's no surprise that Eng.
Sh. Ch. Ferndel Cecilia was top
brood bitch all-breeds in 2004 and
2005 and runner-up in 2003.

THE WELSHIE IN THE UNITED STATES

In the United States the breed was
formally recognized by the
American Kennel Club (AKC) in
1906, although red and white
spaniels had been seen in earlier
illustrations or paintings. The
Mississippi Valley Kennel Club

show (April 1911) recorded an
entry of four Welsh Springer
Spaniels, all owned by Mr. A. A.
Busch.

The first Welsh Springer
Spaniel to be registered was
Faircroft Bob (great-grandson of
Eng. Ch. Longmynd Calon Fach),
owned and bred by Harry B.
Hawes in 1914. His dam,
Faircroft Sue, was registered in

Eng. Sh. Ch.
Ferndel Cecilia
(left) and Eng.
Sh. Ch.
Hillpark Music
of the Night in
1999.

Eng. Sh. Ch.
Dalati Sioni,
1983, a top
producer in
the breed.

1915. Until 1929 only a handful of Welshies were registered and between 1929 and 1949 there were none at all.

This doesn't mean there were no Welsh Springer Spaniels at all, because there were. They were owned by sportsmen as hunting companions and were either unregistered or registered in the American Field Stud Book, a working gundog registry not affiliated with the AKC. Until the 1950s they were acquired, bred and kept purely as working dogs.

One of the early supporters of the breed was Hobart Ames of Connecticut, who imported his shooting dogs from the kennels of A. T. Williams. One of the last of the Llanharan strain, Marged O'Matherne, was imported in 1927 by a sportsman in the Midwest.

Probably the most famous introduction of the breed to America came in 1950 when

SHOW TIME

In the United States, Welsh Springers were being shown ten years before there were classes available for English Springers.

Dorothy Ellis and four of her adult Downland Welsh and a puppy flew from England to New York to exhibit at Westminster, Hartford and Boston. At each show one of her dogs was Best of Breed, and they received much attention and publicity. She went home without the dogs, having sold them to breed fanciers; the first American champion, Ch. Holiday of Happy Hunting, was a son of two of these imports.

In the early '60s, Bert and Edna Randolph of Randhaven kennels owned or bred eight American champions. They also hired a handler to assist them in showing their rare breed. This handler was D. Lawrence (Laddie) Carswell. Laddie imported Eng. Sh. Ch. Trigger of Tregwillym in 1962. He set out to introduce the breed and to educate the judges and the public on the breed, which earned him the nickname "Mr. Welsh Springer Spaniel." When he died in 1995, the breed lost a great expert and staunch supporter.

The Welsh Springer Spaniel Club of America (WSSCA) was founded in 1961, but it was in the 1970s that the breed started

Ch. Fracas Little Caesar, winning Best of Breed at the WSSCA specialty in 1986.

its rise in popularity. Welsh Springers were found across the US. Imports from Brent, Pencelli, Hillpark and Tregwillym molded with American stock to form the foundation for many of today's breeding programs, together with later imports from Scandinavia and the Netherlands. The most influential import has been Dutch and German Ch. Valentijn van Snellestein, who was top producer in 1985.

The first club show was held in 1980, where Best in Show was Ch. Randail Taffy of Sylabru, whose pedigree could be traced back to the Downland dogs. The second time she won Best of Breed at the club show was from the Veteran Class.

In 1986, when the club cele-brated its 25th anniversary, Ch. Fracas Little Caesar, bred and owned by Frances and Carl Bloom, and the son of two British imports, Ch. Hillpark Brutus and Ch. My Fanwy Fair of Hillpark, was Best of Breed. Handled by Laddie Carswell, "Little C" became the first Welsh to win an all-breed Best in Show in America and the first and only one to date to win Best in Show at the American Spaniel Club show, where all spaniel breeds compete. Some 37 years after Dorothy Ellis came to Madison Square Garden, Little C was also the first and only Welsh Springer Spaniel to win a Sporting Group

Ch. Rysan's First Round Kayo CDX, shown winning Best of Breed in 1990.

placement at the Westminster Show in the 20th century.

Ch. Rysan's First Round Kayo CDX, bred and owned by Sandra and Richard Rohrbacher, was a multiple Best in Show winner and Best of Breed twice at the Welsh Springer Spaniel Club national specialty. Ch. Bel Canto's Remington Gunfire also was Best of Breed twice at the national specialty. "Rusty" was bred by Bob and Patricia Ramsey and owned by Lisa and David Hubler.

Another dog who won the national specialty twice was

Ch. Bel Canto's Remington Gunfire, a typical American champion.

Imports that have done a lot of winning and were of great influence on the breed were Ch. Hillpark Caesar, Ch. Hillpark Brutus, Ch. Pencelli Thomas and Ch. Dalati Marc.

Major winners of the new millennium include BIS/BISS Ch. Rolyart's Still The One WD, CGC ("Gator") and BIS/2x BISS Ch. Benton Ivy League OA, OAJ, CGC, FFXG ("Eero"). Highlights of Gator's impressive career include being top Welsh Springer from 1999–2003; 110 Sporting Group placements, with 25 of them Group Ones; many career Bests of Breed and a Best in Show; and Best of Breed twice at Westminster, the WSSCA national specialty and the American Spaniel Club show. Gator is breeder/owner/handled by Shelley Traylor and Cindy Ford.

Eero, owned by Adrienne Bancker of Briarbanc kennels, was the youngest dog and the first Welshie ever to win a national specialty from the classes, doing so at ten-and-a-half months old, and the first undocked Welshie to win a national specialty. He holds many other records for undocked Welsh Springers, including first Group One, first Best in Show and first Best of Breed at the AKC/Eukanuba Invitational. He is now racking up titles in agility, too.

Am./Can. Ch. Brafci's True Colors CD, two-time specialty winner.

Ch. Royailes Kool Ham Luke, pictured following a Best in Show win in 1996.

Am./Can. Ch. Brafci's True Colors CD. Furthermore, he was Best of Breed at the American Spaniel Club, at Westminster and at the national specialty all in one year (1997). In 1999 he won Best of Breed again at the American Spaniel Club from the Veteran Class. "Quincy" was bred by Tonia and Paul Farnell and owned by Marion Daniel.

The most influential sire of the 21st century has been Gator's sire, Ch. Don's Still Waters Run Deep SH, WDX, CGC ("Kalven"). Gator and two of the top-winning Welsh bitches are included in

BIS/BISS Ch. Rolyart's Still The One WD, CGC ("Gator"), breeder/owner/handled by Shelley Traylor and Cindy Ford, is a top winner and record-breaker.

ments, including Best of Breed at the American Spaniel Club's Flushing Spaniel show. Breeder/owner/handled by Anne Legare for much of his show career, he has also produced some top-quality offspring that are now being seen in the ring.

Among the many milestones for BIS/2x BISS Ch. Benton Ivy League OA, OAJ, CGC, FFXG ("Eero"), owned by Adrienne Bancker, is being top Welsh Springer for 2004.

Kalven's 23 champion offspring, who have many impressive wins among them. Kalven was bred in Sweden by Karin Brostam and Annica Högström of the Don's kennels and is owned by Peggy Ruble and Susan Riese.

The number-one Welshie for 2005 was Ch. Holly House Sweet William, having won multiple Bests of Breed and Group place-

At a WSSCA specialty, from left to right: Mrs. Anne Walton, a judge from the UK; Mrs. Marta Stoneman with Ch. Statesman's Llanharan Abbey and Mrs. Susan Riese, WSSCA president and breeder of Abbey.

Eng. Sh. Ch. Tregwillym Golden Gem with breeder Mr. Cliff Payne in 1975. Golden Gem went to Australia in 1978 and became, along with her grandson, the foundation of Nantyderi kennels.

THE WELSH SPRINGER SPANIEL AROUND THE WORLD

The Welsh Springer Spaniel has an international network of breed devotees, who often know each other personally or who keep in touch through the Internet. You will find many international websites and sometimes even a virtual breed show where the dogs are being judged in classes like a real dog show.

AUSTRALIA

We know that some Welsh Springers were exported to Australia before World War II, but no records could be found and it is likely that these dogs were not used for breeding purposes. The real history started in 1973 when Mr. and Mrs. S. Jeffery (Talgarth) imported Plattburn Paceman and Plattburn Pi, bred by Ken Burgess in Great Britain. This successful pair formed the start of the breed in Australia.

Sue and Jim Simmonds (Pennlyon) purchased Talgarth Temptation, who had two litters from which seven puppies later became champions. Talgarth Tasha, litter sister to Temptation, also became a champion, and she produced three Australian champions. All of these litters were sired by Pencelli Prospect, who not only sired 9 litters in which he produced 27 Australian champions and a New Zealand champion but who also was very successful in the ring, winning 16 Groups, a Reserve Best in Show and a Best in Show.

Talgarth Cassandra, owned by Bobbie Hitchcock, was mated to Pencelli Prospect to produce the first Rhiwderin litter, and Tess Hay's Brynderyn kennels were founded on Rhiwderin and Pennlyon stock.

In 1978 Scott and Eira Taylor imported Eng. Sh. Ch. Tregwillym Golden Gem and her grandson Tregwillym Taliesin. These two were the start of the Nantyderi kennels, and these imports can be found in many pedigrees.

In 1982 a breed club was formed. A number of open shows are held annually and since 1989 two championship shows have been held every year. At all-breed championship shows, Welsh Springers have won Best in Group and Best in Show, among them Gr. Ch. Goldmaid Diamond Duke, Gr. Ch. Goldmaid Topaz Terror, Gr. Ch. Tregaron Afon Mynach, Gr. Ch. Goldmaid Strike Me Wild, Gr. Ch. Laugharne Khufuu Al, Ch. Glenquayle Gandalf and Gr. Ch. Slyvkin Tristan.

In the annual competition for show dogs held by *Dogz Online*, an online Australian pure-bred dog community, Gr. Ch. Goldmaid Strike Me Wild was the top Welsh Springer for 2003, 2004 and 2005, and was 15th overall in the Gundog Group for 2005. Dogs are ranked according to points, which are awarded for Best in Show, Reserve Best in Show, Best in Group and Reserve Best in Group wins. In obedience competition, Welshies also do very well in Australia.

Imports into Australia have come mainly from the UK but also from New Zealand, Finland and the Netherlands. The greatest number of Welsh Springers is seen in New South Wales. It is pleasing that every year the number of registered Welshies shows a slight increase.

CANADA

Registered in 1949, the first Welsh Springer Spaniels in Canada were Countess Hobo of Dale and Prince Bohunk, but nothing was heard of them or their owner, Mr. Kirkpatrick of Ontario.

Peggy Saltman (Coedmawr) imported Ceinwen of Tregwillym in 1962, the third Welsh to be registered with the Canadian Kennel Club and the first to gain a championship title. She bought Ghost Inn Peredur, but when all of her attempts to breed Ceinwen to Peredur failed, she imported Tregwillym Merionwen. The resulting three litters were the beginning of her Coedmawr kennel, which proved to be the foundation of several kennels in western Canada and of two-thirds of all Canadian Welsh Springers.

In 1969 Eve Carter of Ontario imported Rona of Pencelli who, in whelp to Nobleman of Tregwillym, became the foundation bitch of her Ghost Inn kennel.

The Roseraie kennel of Andree Plante started in 1975 with two bitches imported from Great Britain and a Coedmawr dog. Six litters were born and most of the puppies were shown. However, in 1977, Andree Plante decided to stop breeding and showing after six of her dogs perished in a fire that destroyed her home.

Bankdam's Taffy Bark was the first champion for Gordon Wilkinson, later followed by Coedmawr Megan of Bankdam and Ch. Pencelli Pandour. Taffy, bred to Megan, produced the top Welsh ever bred in Canada,

Danish Ch. Booze Boleyn van Berkenstein (right) and litter sister Dutch Ch. Blessed Boleyn van Berkenstein (left), bred in the Netherlands by Monique Huis In't Veld.

Am./Can. Ch. Bankdam's Bobby Dazzler, whose influence in the breed is still felt. The top Welshie in Canada in 1993, 1994 and 1995; the top Welshie in the US in 1994 and 1995; the best bitch at the WSSCA national specialty in 1995; and America's top obedience Welsh two years running were all great-grandchildren of Bobby Dazzler.

A milestone for the breed occurred in 1983 when Am./Can. Ch. Killagay's Court Jester became the first Welsh Springer to win an all-breed Best in Show in Canada.

DENMARK

The Hoje Mon kennel, owned by Ingelise and Ivan Selberg, was the first Welsh Springer kennel in Denmark. Ingelise and Ivan imported Maroon Lotta from Sweden and Dalati Denol and Dalati Dyma Fi from Great Britain in 1974 and 1975.

Mette and Lars Kruuse founded the Sweet Chester kennel and Kirsten Hahn and Ove Noraett the Danebod kennel. They imported Triggers Osborne from Sweden and Brynmore and Rosa van Snellestein from the Netherlands, making the breeding foundation in Denmark a combination of Swedish and Dutch bloodlines.

In 1986 Lena Sorenson (Blazewood) got her first Welsh Springer, Sweet Chester's Cliff, from Sweet Chester kennel. She imported Booze Boleyn van Berkenstein in 1990. Booze

Brynmore van Snellestein was imported into Denmark from the Netherlands.

The Danish Triggers Osborne, originally from Sweden.

ples of the dual-purpose Welsh include Danish/Ger./Lux. Ch. Red and White's Surtsey Superior and Danish/Int. Ch. My Welsh Attaboy. Both have excellent working abilities and the latter is, at the time of this writing, the only spaniel to have passed the Danish Kennel Club's new hunting test for retrievers and spaniels. Other dogs achieving success in field trials are Carwyn Our Loyal Welsh and his sister Danish Ch. Chincianetti Our Loyal Welsh, who passed a field-trial test in 2004 and earned her Danish championship at 19 months old.

In January 2005 the Danish Kennel Club set forth that a gundog could become a Danish champion without having passed a working test. This new title is DKUCH, different from the title DKCH for the dog who has passed a field trial as well. One of the dogs to win this title was an import from Sweden, DKUCH Benton It's My Party, who was a World Winner in 2003 and top spaniel in 2004. The first dog ever to become a working champion is Hunting Red Audi, bred and owned by Birgit Pedersen.

FINLAND

Mrs. Misse Puolakkainen was the first to introduce the breed in Finland. She imported two Mustela bitches, two sisters by Plattburn Pimlico, from Sweden in 1967. The first two litters in 1968

became the breed record holder and won a Best in Show at the breed club championship show in the Netherlands.

Birte Bjorn started her Red and White kennel in 1987 with Danebod's Diana Bianca, who was very successful in the show ring and in the field. Merethe Andersen and Finn Nielsen started their Gallois kennel in 1989 and imported Cwrt Afon Harri. Their more recent import from Sweden, Hammalgården's Original and Best, had great influence on the breed in Denmark.

In order to have a new bloodline, in 1991 French Duke des Terres Froides was imported from France. Since then, Welsh Springers have been imported from various countries, and bloodlines vary.

In recent years some Welshies have competed at field trials and some breeders have become more aware of the importance of this dual-purpose dog. Recent exam-

were the beginning of the successful Skyway prefix and the foundation of the breed in Finland. In 1969 she imported Ambassador of Tregwillym, Nobleman of Tregwillym and the bitch Golden Charm of Tregwillym, followed in 1975 by Dalati Dyma Fi, who turned out to be a very good stud dog. His excellent breed type was passed on to many of his successful offspring.

In 1984 Delkens Turul came to Marjo Jaakkola (Benton). He can be considered to be the most important sire in the breed and founder of the breed as it is today in Finland. Not only was he himself a top winner but he also sired over 30 champions. Indeed, Marjo Jaakkola is one of Finland's top breeders.

Two kennels started with Dalati Dyma Fi offspring: Mrs. Tiina Mattila's Rwyn and Terttu and Hannu Suonto's Sprightly. Tiina Mattila can be considered to

be the most successful breeder of Welsh Springer Spaniels in Finland, having bred over 50 champions, many international champions and top winners.

Several champions have come from Sprightly breeding, including Sprightly Xylophone, who was the most successful prize-winning Welsh ever in Finland.

In the 1970s, Tuuliki and Reino Makitalo started the Sinsir kennel with a bitch from Sweden bred on Brent lines. Leila Kärkäs established the Mandeville kennel and bred the champions Roger Ribbons, Ragtime Rudy and Roland Rabbit, all by Ch. Delkens Turul.

While many new breeders have come into the breed, some of the longtime breeders, such as the Rwyn kennels, have unfortunately stopped breeding. Docking has been banned in Finland since 1996, and since 2001 there has also been a ban on the import of docked spaniels.

In the beginning of the new millennium the dominating dogs were Int. Ch. Cleavehill Rhyader and Int. Ch. Benton Everybody Duck, the latter being the product of the first AI (artificial insemination) litter (Arkview Moonstroller x Int. Ch. Benton Garden Party), born in 2003. He became top gundog in Finland in 2005 and made breed history by winning the Reserve Challenge Certificate at England's Crufts show in 2006, being the first foreign Welsh Springer to do so.

SWEDEN

The first Welsh Springer Spaniel in Sweden was Linkhill Five-to-One, who was imported in 1963 by Marianne Hermelin (Mustela). She was a very successful bitch and her first litter with Gay Boy of Tregwillym gave the breed a very good start.

Anita Norberg (Himledalen) imported Tidemarsh Ruff, who had a lot of influence on the breed in Sweden. Mrs. Grant Carlson (Corydon) started in the '60s. She imported four dogs, the most important of whom were Ch. Rebecca of Basildon and Benefactor of Brent.

Catarina Hultgren (Trigger) started in 1971. Trigger Bonny Lass is the only field-trial champion in Sweden. She has been very successful over the years in showing, obedience and field trials.

Pencelli Mwyn, imported into Sweden by Birgitta Thoresson.

Margareta Edman (Clumbrolds) started in 1976 on the lines of Corydon. She imported Welsh Guide of Tregwillym, who was the sire of Int. SFN Ch. Clumbrolds Purpurdöd, the only Swedish Welshie to win Best in Show at an all-breed championship show. He was exported to Finland, where he had a great influence on the breed.

Merry One, the kennel that Bjorn and Yvonne Skeppstedt Schill started in 1985, has been successful in all fields. Carina Arvidsson started the Freckles kennel in 1986 with a Trigger bitch. Freckles Inspiration became the top field-trial dog in the breed

Ch. Don's Thunderstorm was the top Welsh Springer in Sweden in 1993.

Nor. Ch. Metzgard's Moonlight Valley, bred by Rita and Bjorn Roger in Norway and foundation of the Don's kennels in Sweden.

and Freckles Miss Decibell the Best All-Rounder in 1995.

Birgitta Thoresson imported a few of Harold Newman's dogs when he died. The most influential and successful was Pencelli Mwyn, who put a mark on the breed in the '80s. He was a top winner and was twice Best in Show at the club show.

Karin Brostam and Annica Högström of the Don's kennels started in 1989 with Weslave Winter Breeze and Ch. Metzgard's Moonlight Valley, who became

Nor. Ch. Inu-Goya Ferrymaster, multi-Group and Best in Show winner in Norway.

the top-winning Welsh ever in Sweden. He was twice Best in Show at the club show and had several Best in Show wins at championship shows, one of them being the Centenary Show of the Swedish Kennel Club in 1989, the biggest show ever in Sweden. Ch. Don's Thunderstorm was a Group winner and was top Welsh in 1993.

Gudrun Jonsson's Hammalgårdens kennel started in 1990. Hillcrofts was founded in 1990 by Agneta and Bert Mansson. They started with Clumbrolds Trollslanda and have been doing very well. Laila Gistedt started her Designer's kennels in the mid-'90s.

NORWAY
The first Welsh Springer Spaniel came to Norway in 1970, but it was not until the 1980s that serious breeding began, with Rita and Bjørn Gran's Metzgard kennels. They imported Hasselholm's Isabella from Sweden and Delkens Troydon from Englad, and from this combination came their most famous dog, Ch. Metzgard's Moonlight Valley. The Metzgard kennel stopped its activities in the early 1990s, but most of the dogs in Norway have Metzgard dogs in their pedigrees.

The 1980s also saw the start of the Inu-Goya kennel of Frank Bjerklund and Terje Johnsen. Although they mainly bred

English Springers, a fair number of Welshies were bred and shown by them. They imported Eng. Sh. Ch. Ferndel Harvest Gold and Ferndel Fun, but their most influential import was Kazval Call Collect, who is the most winning Welsh in Norway ever.

The top dog in 2000 was Int./Nor. Ch. Kloverengens Emmi, sired by Inu-Goya Roadrunner, himself a son of Kazval Call Collect. "Emmi" is also one of the very few Welshies to compete in agility; in 2005 she was the top agility dog of all spaniel breeds. The top dog in 2003 was sired by the renowned Kazval Call Collect and the top dog in 2005 was sired by Nor. Ch. Ferndel Fun at Inu-Goya.

Registrations show a slight increase, and imports come in fairly frequently, about eight per year. Welsh Springers are seldom seen at field trials in Norway but a few have passed their hunting tests, which is necessary for obtaining the title of International Champion.

Norway does not have "big" breeders; most breeders only breed one or maybe two litters per year. There is no Norwegian breed club for Welsh Springer Spaniels, but there is a club for spaniel breeds.

NETHERLANDS
The first Welsh Springer Spaniel to be registered and shown in the

Dutch Ch. Plattburn Proclaim in 1974.

Netherlands was Mist (Longmynd Morgan x Longmynd Myfandy), born in 1908, bred by Mrs. H. D. Greene. Mist literally disappeared in the mist, because after having been shown a couple of times (and winning his classes), no further traces have been found of him. The next entry in the stud book was a litter registered as English Springers except for one puppy, Good Luck's Boy, who was registered and shown as

Dutch Ch. Dalati Derw, winning at the Dutch championship show in 1979.

Mr. Ken
Burgess of
Plattburn
kennels
(second from
the left),
judging a
Welsh
Springer
Spaniel Club
show in the
Netherlands.

Mr. Ken Burgess of Plattburn kennels (second from the left), judging a Welsh Springer Spaniel Club show in the Netherlands.

a red and white Welsh Springer Spaniel.

    After that we find no more mention of Welsh Springer

Spaniels until 1950, when Red Rascal of Downland, bred by Dorothy Ellis, came to the Netherlands and Mrs. S. E. van

Dutch and German Ch. Valentijn van Snellestein, a very influential import and top producer in 1985.

Boetzelaer imported Rushbrooke Rhoda, bred by Mr. Hal Leopard. Rhoda's first litter by Red Rascal was registered under the Riverland prefix. In the following years the number of Welsh Springers slowly but gradually increased.

Influential imports in those early days were Rushbrooke Ringer, Dalati Delwen and Jonathan of Brent. In the early '70s, Plattburn Pinecone was imported in whelp by Plattburn Perchance. One of the pups, Isselsteyn's Cita, became a champion and produced many more champions mated to Dalati Aled and later to Dutch Ch. Dalati Derw. Another dog that had great influence on the breed was Reliance of Krackton, who sired four champions. The Plattburn kennel of Ken Burgess in Britain

Top Welsh Springer and top gundog in the Netherlands in 1999 was Dutch Ch. Inma's Nimble Nidian, bred and owned by Ine van de Beuken.

contributed significantly to the foundation of the breed in the Netherlands. Later quality imports from Pencelli and Dalati helped to build the breed.

One of the most important kennels was undoubtedly Ria Lissenberg-Hörter's (now Hörter) Van Snellestein. Her success started with the import of Eng. Sh. Ch. Bramblebank Calamity Jane (later a Dutch champion as well) in 1978. She represented a different type of Welsh Springer and offered a much-needed new bloodline. Isselsteyn's Iris (Dalati Aled x Isselsteyn's Cita) mated to Lennart of Speldermark produced the first Snellestein champion. The second champion was Valentijn van Snellestein (Reliance of Krackton x Bramblebank Calamity Jane). He went to the United States in the mid-'80s, where he had a successful show career and proved to be a valuable stud dog.

Eng. Sh. Ch./Dutch Ch. Bramblebank Calamity Jane, bred by Mrs. V. Roach and later owned by Mrs. Ria Hörter, here seen winning at Crufts in 1978.

The first Welsh Springer to win a Best in Show in the Netherlands: Multi-Ch. Northoaks Sea Sun Flower, owned by Marie Madeleine van Grinsven.

The top Dutch Welsh Springer for three consecutive years was Dutch Ch. Nyliram Mr. Dark Horse, bred by Mr. T. Graham in Great Britain and owned by Mrs. Ria Hörter.

Dutch and Luxembourg Ch. Nicolaas van Snellestein in the mid-1980s.

The top Welsh Springer in the Netherlands in 1998 was Dutch Ch. Wesley of Rowan's Residence, bred and owned by Mrs. Ria Hörter.

He came back after a couple of years to resume his successful show career as a veteran. Ria stopped her breeding in 1984 but came back a few years later with her new prefix (of Rowan's Residence) and regained her position as one of the top Dutch breeders. Her greatest success came with the import Dutch Ch. Nyliram Mr. Dark Horse (by Eng. Sh. Ch. Russethill Royal Salute over Nyliram), who was top Welsh Springer in the Netherlands for three years.

Monique Huis In't Veld (van Berkenstein kennel) had a very good start with Wainfelin Miss Money Penny. Over the years this kennel has produced a number of top-winning Welsh Springers and several champions.

A more recent kennel is Inma's. Owner Ine van den Beuken bred her first litter in

1987. She is one of the most successful breeders in the Netherlands, having bred quite a number of champions. Her top-winning bitch to date is Dutch Ch. Inma's Nimble Nidian.

Another successful breeder is Marie Madeleine van Grinsven (Of the Yasmin Garden), who bred her first litter in 1988. She has bred several champions, but her greatest success came with the import Northoaks Sea Sun Flower, who won many titles and was the first Welsh Springer to win a Best in Show at an all-breed championship show in the Netherlands.

This feat was repeated by Inma's Valuable Vivian, who was Best in Show in Maastricht in September 2002. Inma's Welshies have become very successful: Dutch Ch. Inma's Nimble Nidian is the all-time top-winning bitch with five Groups and two Reserve Bests in Show, and Inma's Vital Flip is the first Dutch Welsh Springer to win the Group at a World Show (Dortmund, Germany in 2003). The two most influential recent imports are Red Ryan des Terres Froides (bred by Brigitte Bolze in France) and Benton Kansas Storm.

Fortunately, there is a growing interest in the working side of the breed, and two Welsh Springers have succeeded in winning the prestigious title of

Niclas van Snellestein (brother of Nicolaas) went to the United States, where he became an American champion.

International Champion through their achievements in conformation and field trials.

FRANCE
The first breeder of Welsh Springer Spaniels in France was Dr. Drouillard, a Cocker Spaniel breeder who imported Peridot of Tarbay in whelp to Sh. Ch. Mikado of Broomleaf in 1958. The bitch Hilda du Valcain went to L. R. Veignat, who bred her to Myrddin Dewr. A bitch from that combination, Merry des Fretillants, was bred to Deri Day of Linkhill and produced Pat and Porros des Frétillants and Quetzal des Frétillants in a repeat mating. They were all very successful in the show ring and in the field.

Sharlotte des Frétillants went to Brigitte Bolze (des Terres

From France, a group of Welshies "Des Frétillants," bred and owned by Mr. L. R. Veignat in 1980.

There is an official spaniel club, and Welsh Springer breeders also have formed their own club (www.broussailleurs.com). Working ability is held in high regard and French breeders are very careful to preserve the dual purpose of the breed. The French Welsh Springers are of top quality.

GERMANY
The Welsh Springer has never been a popular breed in Germany and it is only in recent years that interest in the breed has developed. In the '60s and '70s it was mainly Harry Hinckeldeyn (Hinckeldeyn's) and Renate Wulff (von der Grauen Stadt) who kept the breed going. Jürgen and Lucy

Froides). Her offspring were very successful in the ring and did a lot to help the breed along.

The most influential dog in recent years has been Safran d'Ann Cambris, who is a Dual Champion (Show Champion as well as Field-Trial Champion).

French and International Ch. Chadock des Terres Froides, bred and owned by Mrs. Brigitte Bolze.

Wallat started their von der Ruraue kennel in the early '90s and they successfully try to combine show quality and working ability in their breeding program. Nowadays Welsh Springers are seen more often at shows, although not in any great numbers, and there are some imports, mainly from Denmark.

CZECH REPUBLIC

Welsh Springer history in the Czech Republic started in 1963 when Mr. Liml imported Hinckeldeyn's Aar (out of Rushbrooke Ringlet) and received Bright Poppet of Hearts, bred in Great Britain, from Mr. Hinckeldeyn in Germany. This pair had three litters.

Later Hinckeldeyn's Elk (from Germany) and Ugo des Frétillants (from France) came to the country. In the following years more dogs were imported from France, Holland and Sweden.

Since the right to be a breeder was reserved to members of the Union of Czech Hunters, the number of litters was restricted

and almost entirely confined to hunters.

Nowadays, traveling is easier and dogs from other countries are used more frequently. By making a test for hunting suitability obligatory for dogs that are being used for breeding, the breeders have succeeded in preserving the working abilities of the breed and Czech puppies, especially from the Jifex kennels, find their way to working and showing enthusiasts in other countries.

ABOVE: German, Luxembourg and International Ch. Gaston von der Ruraue (left) and German, Luxembourg, Polish and International Ch. Jasmin von der Ruraue, bred and owned by Lucy and Jurgen Wallat in Germany. LEFT: A stamp issued by the Central African Republic that honors the *Springer Gallois*—the Welsh Springer Spaniel.

REPUBLIQUE CENTRAFRIQUE

175f

POSTES 199

SPRINGER GALLOIS

WORLDWIDE APPEAL

With his temperament and character, his pearly white and red coat, his handy size and general appearance, it is no wonder that so many people in so many countries consider the Welsh Springer Spaniel as one of the most attractive dogs in the world.

CHARACTERISTICS OF THE
WELSH SPRINGER SPANIEL

PHYSICAL CHARACTERISTICS

The Welsh Springer Spaniel is a medium-sized, symmetrical, compact dog, and his build is meant for hard work. He is a proper working dog and, as such, has a lot of energy and endurance. His temperament is merry and active, interested in everything that happens, although he is always gentle and never aggressive. It goes without saying that a dog with such a temperament can never be happy in the confines of a small apartment with an owner who is at work all day. Such a dog needs the liveliness of a family and lots of exercise.

Welshies love to be around their owners and are always ready for a cuddle!

The Welsh Springer has several very distinct characteristics. First of all, his color: rich red and white only, a beautiful combination of a deep and warm red and the purest white possible. That means that any shade of orange, brown or yellow is wrong. The pattern of the markings and the quantity of red markings is totally unimportant and just a matter of taste, although for a show dog "unfortunate" markings may be a slight handicap. Some people prefer open markings, but saddle-marked dogs are quite often seen and are just as attractive.

Another characteristic is his outline: rectangular, compact and slightly arched over the loin. There is little essential difference between the bodies in many varieties of spaniel, apart from this slight arch over the loin. This is a result of the propulsion from the rear, a muscular development, and should not be confused with a roached back or a rise toward the rear. Any arch in a different place means that the dog has either a dip behind the shoulder or an uphill rise in the rear. The correct outline is a very important characteristic which—together with his

After a successful day in the ring with a Best of Breed win, Thomas cools off and has some fun at "Dog Beach," a popular spot in Huntington Beach, California.

lovely color—distinguishes the Welsh Springer from the other spaniels.

Another distinctive feature is his head, which is very balanced, beautifully chiseled and with eyes that may vary from hazel to dark but must always have that gentle spaniel expression. The ear should be vineleaf-shaped. The ear size may vary, but for practical reasons a comparatively small ear is preferred.

Fortunately, there is not yet a divergence in type between the working Welshie and the show Welshie. The difference is not as great as that in English Springers or Cockers, for example, and breeders are trying very hard to combine type and working instincts. Many trainers have reached dual-purpose success, but it is a dilemma to try and breed for conservation of working instincts, type and soundness.

Why the breed is fortunate enough not to have a separation of working and show type is not quite clear. It could be because the breed is numerically small and not very fashionable and because there is a good understanding between the working and showing fraternity. Also, there is a great deal of determination on the part of many Welsh Springer owners and breeders to aim for the dual-purpose ideal in countries around the world.

A gundog by nature, the Welsh Springer loves and needs activity. A supervised run through a field or in the woods will keep him physically fit and mentally stimulated.

WELSH SPRINGER PERSONALITY

The Welsh Springer Spaniel is a gundog although he is used less for work nowadays. That doesn't mean, however, that he has lost his working abilities. In many countries people are still training and working their Welshies, and although they have to compete against their talented English Springer cousins, often from working lines, they do manage to hold their own.

Gundogs in general are docile, trainable, ready to serve, loyal and faithful, and they love to be with their humans. They are absolutely devoted to their families. That means that a Welshie should live in the house and be around family members as much as possible. He can be left on his own for several hours when the need arises but only when he has become accustomed to an empty house.

Being a gundog means that a Welsh Springer needs exercise and the excitement of running in a field or the woods and smelling all sorts of highly exciting smells. This will keep him healthy not only physically but mentally as well. A gentle stroll in the park is definitely not enough for a dog with so much stamina and such a strong scenting ability. A Welsh Springer is an alert and intelligent dog with an inquiring mind, which means that he can be quite lively and high-spirited. Not only does he require plenty of exercise but also training and education. If his liveliness is not channeled, you may end up with a dog who is mischievous and destructive, traits that you may find very difficult or even impossible to cure. A dog that has plenty of exercise of body and mind will be a happy, relaxed dog in the house who, after his exercise, will love to be curled up near you (preferably on the couch, of course!).

A well-trained Welshie makes a very good pet. He loves company and is very good with children and other dogs. He may be a bit reserved with strangers, but he will never show aggressiveness towards them. His happy temperament with the ever-wagging tail makes him fun to be with. However, it should never be forgotten that a Welshie is a spaniel; therefore, obedience may not be one of his stronger points. A gentle but firm hand is an absolute necessity.

You may find there are two types of Welsh Springers: the quiet, friendly and sometimes

rather reserved or withdrawn dog or the outgoing, exuberant, very active and noisy dog, always friendly and non-aggressive. It goes without saying that dogs of such different temperaments need different training methods.

Welsh Springers do love to play and they have a sense of humor. He may look gloomy or downright sad with his spaniel face but he never really is, and he delights in fun and play. He loves to play tug-of-war and hide-and-seek, and you can easily teach him basic commands like sit and stay without his even noticing it!

Your Welshie will love to learn and play retrieving games because he loves to carry things in his mouth. Don't punish him for going off with your shoe, but take it gently from him and thank him profusely for giving it back to you. You'll find that after a while he will bring everything he finds back to you and be very proud of it as well. It may be a bit of a

Young puppies and young children go together naturally—just be sure that they both know how to behave properly with each other.

Ch. Meke Aloha O'Killagay, living the life of luxury as she catches some rays on vacation in Florida.

The best of friends—a handsome young Welshie with his handsome young master.

very positive traits that can turn negative if not used in the right way. Loyalty and protectiveness can turn into sharpness, especially towards other dogs; caution towards strangers can turn into shyness or the capacity to be easily frightened; liveliness can turn into excitability and near hysteria or a very noisy animal. Everything really depends on you. Your behavior and the training you give your dog will determine the kind of dog you are going to have in the future.

nuisance, having to put back everything where it belongs, but it will teach your dog to retrieve without his realizing it. It will also teach you not to leave anything precious or fragile where he can pick it up and carry it off!

Energy, liveliness, sensitivity, a sense of humor: these are all

Owners do tend to forget this. They come home with this adorable and sweet puppy, with his cute little face. However, this very sweet puppy sets out to discover how far he can go, what is allowed and what is not. Moreover, if you allow him to get away with everything in the beginning, you will have a very hard time trying to correct his

The loyal and loving Welsh will enjoy accompanying you on your journeys.

behavior. So be wise and keep a tight rein right from the start. Mind you, a tight rein doesn't mean punishment, it just means discipline, i.e., being firm and consistent. Teach the puppy the basics for his good behavior and safety, such as to come back when called and to walk on a lead without pulling.

A Welsh Springer may bark to warn you that there is something wrong (in his eyes), but don't expect him to be a guard dog. He will let you know with a lot of noise that there is a burglar in the house but, having done that, he will happily show the burglar where you keep the silver.

Bearing in mind the two different kinds of temperament, you have to decide, before you set out to buy a puppy, which type in general you would prefer and what activities you are planning to enjoy with your Welshie. Another consideration is that the difference between a dog and bitch is very obvious. A dog is bigger, heavier in bone and in head, whereas a bitch is more refined and elegant. The difference in temperament is not so obvious. Whereas dogs have the reputation of being more difficult, you may find that your dog is a softie and prefers to sleep on your lap. The bitch might be more intolerant and not as even-tempered as the dog. It depends more on the individual. Therefore,

Julita Rainspeckle demonstrates what a Welshie does best.

the only decisive factor in choosing a dog or a bitch is your personal preference.

When buying a Welshie you should realize that he sheds his lovely white and red coat twice a year (some dogs do this the whole year 'round) and the white hairs, in particular, are hard to overlook on your dark blue suit.

His nails have to be trimmed and his ears have to be checked on a regular basis. The Welsh Springer Spaniel's ears are smaller and finer than those of the other spaniel varieties and they do not tend to cause problems, provided that they are regularly checked,

good in obedience and others are even used as therapy dogs for children, elderly or ill people. Yet whatever their task in life, they love doing it and their general attitude is that life is great fun.

Perhaps the first lines of the poem *Ode to the Welsh Springer Spaniel* by Raynor Jacobs help encapsulate the essence of the breed:

A dog for all seasons, Ch. Holly House Empres Josephine enjoys a romp in the snow.

cleaned and kept trimmed on the inside.

Although few of today's Welsh Springer Spaniels are used as hunting companions, many are used for all kinds of activities besides field work. They love agility and flyball, some are quite

They asked me what a Welsh
   Springer was:
It's a working dog, I said.
A dog with chestnut, fox-bright
   coat
With Llanharan spot on head.
A dog with trimming brilliant
   white

Welshies are, in general, healthy dogs and can live good long lifespans. Phoebe, pictured second from the right, was 13 years old when this photo was taken.

And tail quite short, and merry.
A dog to love, and love me too
And bark when necessary.

BREED-SPECIFIC HEALTH CONSIDERATIONS

Although the Welsh Springer Spaniel is a healthy breed, there are a few breed-related hereditary conditions. Responsible breeders will have their stock examined for these conditions and will not breed from affected stock.

Hip dysplasia is a degeneration of the hip socket into which the femoral head rests. The condition is common in most medium to large dogs, and most breeders have x-ray testing done on their breeding stock to avoid breeding from affected dogs. In many countries the x-raying is obligatory if you want to breed, and results are often published by the breed club. In the US, the Orthopedic Foundation for Animals (OFA) evaluates hip x-rays, maintains a registry of dogs' hip status and issues clearances to dogs with healthy hips. Potential owners should ask to see clearances on their pups' parents.

Epilepsy is a condition that is caused by a recessive gene and is very hard to eliminate. Breeders will certainly not breed from affected stock and will be very careful in using close relatives of affected dogs for breeding.

Eye diseases include hereditary cataracts and goniodys-

Welshies love to spend time with young friends and the feeling is mutual. Justin and his dog Ch. Bu-Gwyn Keepin in Fashion always enjoy snuggle time.

genesis. A cataract is a condition in which there is an opacity of the lens and/or capsule. It is often seen in older dogs (ten years and older). Since aging is a gradual process, it is not much cause for concern when a cataract begins to form. However, hereditary cataracts may be a non-congenital defect and can occur at an early age, affecting the eyesight of the dog; therefore, it is much more serious.

Goniodysgenesis is the predisposing abnormality to primary angle-closure glaucoma. It is a congenital defect.

Hypothyroidism is a disorder of the thyroid gland in the neck. Adult dogs are usually affected and may show various symptoms such as lethargy, weight gain, dry skin, puppy-like haircoat and bacterial infections. Once diagnosed, it can be treated with daily medication.

THE AMERICAN KENNEL CLUB BREED STANDARD FOR THE WELSH SPRINGER SPANIEL

GENERAL APPEARANCE

The Welsh Springer Spaniel is a dog of distinct variety and ancient origin, who derives his name from his hunting style and not his relationship to other breeds. He is an attractive dog of handy size, exhibiting substance without coarseness. He is compact, not leggy, obviously built for hard work and endurance. The Welsh Springer Spaniel gives the impression of length due to obliquely angled forequarters and well developed hindquarters. Being a hunting dog, he should be shown in hard muscled working condition. His coat should not be so excessive as to hinder his work as an active flushing spaniel, but should be thick enough to protect him from heavy cover and weather.

SIZE, PROPORTION, SUBSTANCE

A dog is ideally 18–19 inches in height at the withers and a bitch is 17–18 inches at the withers. Any animal above or below the ideal to be proportionately penalized.

Weight should be in proportion to height and overall balance. Length of body from the withers to the base of the tail is very slightly greater than the distance from the withers to the ground. This body length may be the same as the height but never shorter, thus preserving the rectangular silhouette of the Welsh Springer Spaniel.

HEAD

The Welsh Springer Spaniel head is unique and should in no way approximate that of other spaniel breeds. Its overall balance is of primary importance. Head is in proportion to body, never so broad as to appear coarse nor so narrow as to appear racy. The skull is of medium length, slightly domed, with a clearly defined stop. It is well chiseled below the eyes. The top plane of the skull is very slightly divergent from that of the muzzle, but with no tendency toward a down-faced appearance. A short chubby head is most objectionable.

Eyes should be oval in shape, dark to medium brown in color with a soft expression. Preference is for a darker eye though lighter shades of brown are acceptable.

Yellow or mean-looking eyes are to be heavily penalized. Medium in size, they are neither prominent, nor sunken, nor do they show haw. Eye rims are tight and dark pigmentation is preferred.

Ears are set on approximately at eye level and hang close to the cheeks. Comparatively small, the leather does not reach to the nose. Gradually narrowing toward the tip, they are shaped somewhat like a vine leaf and are lightly feathered.

The length of the *muzzle* is approximately equal to, but never longer than that of the skull. It is straight, fairly square and free from excessive flew. Nostrils are well developed and black or any shade of brown in color. A pink nose is to be severely penalized. A scissors *bite* is preferred. An undershot jaw is to be severely penalized.

NECK, TOPLINE, BODY
The *neck* is long and slightly arched, clean in throat and set into

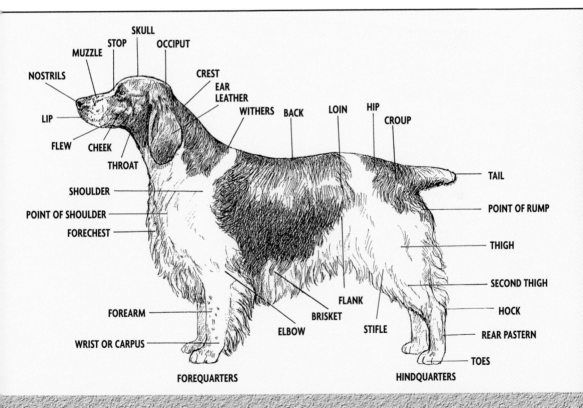

PHYSICAL STRUCTURE OF THE WELSH SPRINGER SPANIEL

long, sloping shoulders. *Topline* is level. The loin is slightly arched, muscular and close-coupled. The croup is very slightly rounded, never steep nor falling off. The topline in combination with proper angulation fore and aft presents a silhouette that appears rectangular. The *chest* is well developed and muscular with a prominent forechest, the ribs well sprung and the brisket reaching to the elbows. The *tail* is an extension of the topline. Carriage is nearly horizontal or slightly elevated when the dog is excited. The tail is generally docked and displays a lively action.

DISTINGUISHABLE TOPLINE
His topline distinguishes the Welsh Springer Spaniel from all of the other spaniel varieties.

FOREQUARTERS

The shoulder blade and upper arm are approximately equal in length. The upper arm is set well back, joining the shoulder blade with sufficient angulation to place the elbow beneath the highest point of the shoulder blade when standing. The forearms are of medium length, straight and moderately feathered. The legs are well boned but not to the extent of coarseness. The Welsh Springer Spaniel's elbows should be close to the body and its pasterns short and slightly sloping. Height to the elbows is approximately equal to the distance from the elbows to the top of the shoulder blades. Dewclaws are generally removed. Feet should be round, tight and well arched with thick pads.

HINDQUARTERS

The hindquarters must be strong, muscular and well boned, but not coarse. When viewed in profile the thighs should be wide and the second thighs well developed. The angulation of the pelvis and femur corresponds to that of the shoulder and upper arm. Bend of stifle is moderate. The bones from the hocks to the pads are short with a well angulated hock joint. When viewed from the side or rear they are perpendicular to the ground. Rear dewclaws are removed. Feet as in front.

COAT

The coat is naturally straight, flat and soft to the touch, never wiry

The major influential sire of the new millennium, Ch. Don's Still Waters Run Deep SH, WDX, CGC, has passed his outstanding type onto his offspring, among them 23 champions who have racked up impressive wins.

or wavy. It is sufficiently dense to be waterproof, thornproof and weatherproof. The back of the forelegs, the hind legs above the hocks, chest and underside of the body are moderately feathered. The ears and tail are lightly feathered. Coat so excessive as to be a hindrance in the field is to be discouraged. Obvious barbering is to be avoided as well.

COLOR
The color is rich red and white only. Any pattern is acceptable and any white area may be flecked with red ticking.

GAIT
The Welsh Springer moves with a smooth, powerful, ground covering action that displays drive from the rear. Viewed from the side, he exhibits a strong forward stride with a reach that does not waste energy. When viewed from the front, the legs should appear to move forward in an effortless manner with no tendency for the feet to cross over or interfere with each other. Viewed from the rear, the hocks should follow on a line with the forelegs, neither too widely nor too closely spaced. As the speed increases the feet tend to converge towards a center line.

TEMPERAMENT
The Welsh Springer Spaniel is an active dog displaying a loyal and affectionate disposition. Although reserved with strangers, he is not timid, shy nor unfriendly. To this day he remains a devoted family member and hunting companion.

Approved June 13, 1989
Effective August 1, 1989

LLANHARAN SPOT
The lozenge-shaped red spot so often found on top of the head between the ears is traditionally called the Llanharan spot because Colonel Blandy-Jenkins's Llanharan Welsh Springer Spaniels often had a spot like that. The Llanharan name lives on!

FINDING A BREEDER

If, after all of the information you have amassed about the breed, you are quite sure that you definitely want a Welsh Springer Spaniel, you have to ask yourself if you can give a Welsh Springer the life he needs. Will you be able to give him all the exercise he requires? Are you willing to spend time with him just playing or sharing activities such as agility or flyball? If you want a hunting companion, are you prepared to train him for work and can you take him on a shoot? Whatever you are going to do with your Welshie, you will have to give him basic obedience training and you may have to go to classes to do so.

Bearing in mind the differences in temperament you may encounter, have you decided which type of temperament suits you best? If you have thought all this out and still believe that a Welsh Springer Spaniel is for you, then your next step is to find a reputable breeder.

It may help you to visit a couple of all-breed dog shows or a specialty show, for Welshies only. Watch the breeders and how

they communicate with their dogs. Look at the dogs and see which breeders have Welshies with the type and temperament you like. You can also contact the Welsh Springer Spaniel Club of America (www.wssca.com) for the contact information of their member breeders in your region. Members must abide by the club's code of ethics, which includes guidelines for responsible breeding.

If you visit a breeder and you are a bit doubtful about the puppies, the breeder or the conditions in which the puppies are kept, or if the breeder thinks that testing for hereditary defects is not necessary, do not buy the puppy! You must be 100% sure— buying because you are afraid to say no or because you feel sorry for the pup is wrong. After all, you are going to buy a companion for the next 12 to 14 years and you must be absolutely sure that he is the one you want and no other!

Should you want to buy a puppy for showing, discuss this with the breeder. The same goes for a future working dog. Also discuss with him what to do in case the puppy will not be show-able. Unforeseen changes may happen as the pup grows, such as a bite that goes wrong. If it is a male, he may turn out to be monorchid (only one descended testicle), etc. If you are very deter-mined to have a show-quality pup, you might do better to buy a more mature puppy, say six to seven months old, so that these risks cannot occur.

Nowadays puppies are often sold with sales contracts. This is fine, but do not sign on the spot. Before you proceed with your purchase, ask the breeder if you can take the contract home to read it carefully so that you know

exactly what you are going to sign. Just as important as a sales contract is a good relationship between you and the breeder. A responsible, dedicated breeder will always be willing to answer all your questions, to calm your fears and to share your joys throughout your Welshie's life.

SELECTING A PUPPY

You have found the breeder who has the type of Welsh Springer you like, and you feel that you can trust him. He lets you know when he has a litter available and there you are, surrounded by all these lovely puppies. How will you ever be able to choose? It is

A proud mother and her litter. These pups will not be ready to go to new homes until they are around eight weeks old.

very tempting to let one of them choose you, but remember that this is not the best approach. Try to make your choice by a process of elimination. If you have decided that you want a bitch puppy, ask the breeder to take

THE FAMILY TREE

Your puppy's pedigree is his family tree. Just as a child may resemble his parents and grandparents, so too will a puppy reflect the qualities, good and bad, of his ancestors, especially those in the first two generations. Therefore it's important to know as much as possible about a puppy's immediate relatives. Reputable and experienced breeders should be able to explain the pedigree and why they chose to breed from the particular dogs they used.

the male puppies away to make it a bit easier to choose. The litter usually contains a range of temperaments from the boisterous and bossy to the shy and submissive. Novice dog owners are best advised to choose a puppy whose temperament is somewhere in the middle. For selection purposes, ask the breeder to take the shy and the bossy puppies away. Now what you are looking for is a healthy, good-looking, happy little thing that, when you crouch down, will in no time be all over you, thinking you are great fun. Ask the breeder if you can meet the litter's dam (and sire if possible) and see what her temperament is like. Discuss the pedigree with him so that you can make sure that your puppy comes from good stock.

Pups usually go to new homes between eight and ten weeks old. A ten-week-old Welsh Springer puppy should have a balanced head with a well-defined stop, a good reach of neck, good ribs and good, well-boned quarters with hocks well let down. Shoulders should be laid back, front legs straight. The feet should be catlike with thick pads. The set of the tail should be a little below the level of the back, and the tail should be carried straight with lively action. The puppy should have nice hazel or dark eyes. A good shiny coat is an indication of good health, as is a happy and exuberant temperament. The color should be a rich red and white.

Here is a useful basic checklist for your new puppy:
- check that the puppy is alert and responsive to sounds;
- ensure that the puppy has no discharge from the eyes or nose;
- check for sores, bald patches or scabs;
- check the puppy's stomach—if distended, it could indicate the wrong diet or worms;
- check for signs of illness such as coughing;
- check that the puppy looks well on the day of collection—if not, arrange to return later;
- ask the breeder when the puppy was last wormed and when he should be wormed again;
- ask the breeder about the vaccination program;
- check whether the breeder would be willing to take the puppy back should this be necessary.

It may seem like a lot of effort and it will be very difficult to withstand all those appealing little spaniel faces, but you have to remember that you cannot be too careful when it comes to deciding on the type of dog you want and finding out about your prospective pup's background. Buying a puppy is not—and should not be—just another

SIGNS OF A HEALTHY PUPPY
Healthy puppies are robust little fellows who are alert and active, sporting shiny coats and supple skin. They should not appear lethargic, bloated or pot-bellied, nor should they have flaky skin or runny or crusted eyes or noses. Their stools should be firm and well formed, with no evidence of blood or mucus.

whimsical purchase. In fact, this is one instance in which you actually do get to choose your own family!

A COMMITTED NEW OWNER
By now you should understand what makes the Welsh Springer Spaniel a most unique and special dog, one that may fit nicely into your family and lifestyle. If you have researched breeders, you should be able to recognize a knowledgeable and

responsible Welsh Springer Spaniel breeder who cares not only about his pups but also about what kind of owner you will be. If you have taken the next step in your new journey, you have found a litter, or possibly two, of quality Welsh Springer Spaniel pups.

A visit with the puppies and their breeder should be an education in itself. Breed research, breeder selection and puppy visitation are very important aspects of finding the puppy of your dreams. Beyond that, these things also lay the foundation for a successful future with your pup. We've mentioned that puppy personalities within each litter vary, from the shy and easygoing puppy to the one who is dominant and assertive, with other pups falling somewhere in

Two adorable three-week-old Welshie pups.

SELECTING FROM THE LITTER

Before you visit a litter of puppies, promise yourself that you won't fall for the first pretty face you see! Decide on your goals for your puppy—show prospect, hunting dog, obedience competitor, family companion—and then look for a puppy who displays the appropriate qualities. In most litters, there is an alpha pup (the bossy puppy) and occasionally a shy fellow who is less confident, with the rest of the litter falling somewhere in the middle. "Middle-of-the-roaders" are safe bets for most families and novice competitors.

between. By spending time with the puppies you will be able to recognize certain behaviors and what these behaviors indicate about each pup's temperament. Which type of pup will complement your family dynamics is best determined by observing the puppies in action within their "pack." Your breeder's expertise and recommendations are so valuable. The breeder's experience in rearing Welsh Springer Spaniel pups and matching their temperaments with appropriate humans offers the best assurance that your pup will meet your needs and expectations. The type of puppy that you select is just as important as your decision that the Welsh Springer Spaniel is the breed for you.

The decision to live with a

Welsh Springer Spaniel is a serious commitment and not one to be taken lightly. This puppy is a living sentient being that will be dependent on you for basic survival for his entire life. Beyond the basics of survival—food, water, shelter and protection—he needs much, much more. The new pup needs love, nurturing and a proper canine education to mold him into a responsible, well-behaved canine citizen. Your Welsh Springer Spaniel's health and good manners will need consistent monitoring and regular "tune-ups," so your job as a responsible dog owner will be ongoing throughout every stage of his life. If you are not prepared to accept these responsibilities and commit to them for the dog's entire life, then you are not prepared to own a dog of any breed.

Although the responsibilities of owning a dog may at times tax your patience, the joy of living with your Welsh Springer Spaniel far outweighs the workload, and a well-mannered adult dog is worth your time and effort. Before your very eyes, your new charge will grow up to be your most loyal friend, devoted to you unconditionally.

YOUR WELSH SPRINGER SPANIEL SHOPPING LIST

Just as expectant parents prepare a nursery for their baby, so

GETTING ACQUAINTED
When visiting a litter, ask the breeder for suggestions on how best to interact with the puppies. If possible, get right into the middle of the pack and sit down with them. Observe which pups climb into your lap and which ones shy away. Toss a toy for them to chase and bring back to you. It's easy to fall in love with the first puppy who picks you, but keep your future objectives in mind before you make your final decision.

should you ready your home for the arrival of your Welsh Springer Spaniel pup. If you have the necessary puppy supplies purchased and in place before he comes home, it will ease the puppy's transition from the warmth and familiarity of his mom and littermates to the brand-new environment of his

A tiny newborn Welsh Springer Spaniel.

popular, but consider how often you will have to pick up those heavy bowls. Buy adult-sized bowls, as your puppy will grow into them before you know it.

THE DOG CRATE

If you think that crates are tools of punishment and confinement

new home and human family. You will be too busy to stock up and prepare your house after your pup comes home, that's for sure! Imagine how a pup must feel upon being transported to a strange new place. It's up to you to comfort him and to let your little pup know that he is going to be happy with you!

FOOD AND WATER BOWLS

Your puppy will need separate bowls for his food and water. Stainless steel bowls are good, but the sturdy special spaniel bowls whose shape allows the dog's ears to fall outside the bowl are popular choices. These bowls save you messy ears after food consumption and a wet floor after drinking! Plastic bowls are very chewable and therefore not advisable. Heavy-duty ceramic bowls are

PEDIGREE VS. REGISTRATION CERTIFICATE

Too often new owners are confused between these two important documents. Your puppy's pedigree, essentially a family tree, is a written record of a dog's genealogy of three generations or more. The pedigree will show you the names as well as performance titles of all dogs in your pup's background. Your breeder must provide you with a registration application, with his part properly filled out. You must complete the application and send it to the AKC with the proper fee. Every puppy must come from a litter that has been AKC-registered by the breeder, born in the US and from a sire and dam that are also registered with the AKC.

The seller must provide you with complete records to identify the puppy. The AKC requires that the seller provide the buyer with the following: breed; sex, color and markings; date of birth; litter number (when available); names and registration numbers of the parents; breeder's name; and date sold or delivered.

for when a dog has misbehaved, think again. Most breeders and almost all trainers recommend a crate as the preferred house-training aid as well as for all-around puppy training and safety. Because dogs are natural den creatures that prefer cave-like environments, the benefits of crate use are many. The crate provides the puppy with his very own "safe house," a cozy place to sleep, take a break or seek comfort with a favorite toy; a travel aid to house your dog when on the road, at motels or at the vet's office; a training aid to help teach your puppy proper toileting habits; and a place of solitude when non-dog people happen to drop by and don't want a lively puppy—or even a

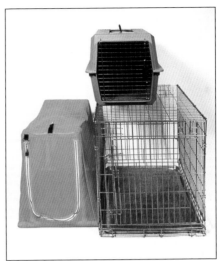

The three most popular crate types: mesh on the left, wire on the right and fiberglass on top.

well-behaved adult dog—saying hello or begging for attention.

Crates come in several types, although the wire crate and the fiberglass airline-type crate are the most popular. Both are safe and your puppy will adjust to either one, so the choice is up to you. The wire crates offer better visibility for the pup as well as better ventilation. Many of the wire crates easily fold into suitcase-size carriers. The fiberglass crates, similar to those used by the airlines for animal transport, are sturdier and more den-like. However, the fiberglass crates do not fold down and are less ventilated than wire crates; this can be problematic in hot weather. Some of the newer crates are made of heavy plastic mesh; they are very lightweight and fold up into slim-line suitcases. However, a mesh

KEEP OUT OF REACH

Most dogs don't browse around your medicine cabinet, but accidents do happen! The drug acetaminophen, the active ingredient in certain popular over-the-counter pain relievers, can be deadly to dogs and cats if ingested in large quantities. Acetaminophen toxicity, caused by the dog's swallowing 15 to 20 tablets, can be manifested in abdominal pains within a day or two of ingestion, as well as liver damage. If you suspect your dog has swiped a bottle of medication, get the dog to the vet immediately so that the vet can induce vomiting and cleanse the dog's stomach.

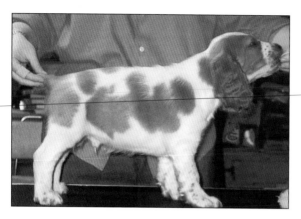

trained and out of the early chewing stage, you can replace the puppy bedding with a permanent crate pad if you prefer. Crate pads and other dog beds run the gamut from inexpensive to high-end doggie-designer styles, but don't splurge on the good stuff until you are sure that your puppy is reliable and won't tear it up or make a mess on it.

PUPPY TOYS

Just as infants and older children require objects to stimulate their minds and bodies, puppies need toys to entertain their curious brains, wiggly paws and achy teeth. A fun array of safe doggie toys will help satisfy your puppy's chewing instincts and distract him from gnawing on the leg of your antique chair or your new leather sofa. Most puppy toys are cute and look as if they would be a lot of fun, but not all are necessarily safe

crate might not be suitable for a pup with manic chewing habits.

Don't bother with a puppy-sized crate. Although your Welsh Springer Spaniel will be a wee fellow when you bring him home, he will grow up in the blink of an eye and your puppy crate will be useless. Purchase a crate that will accommodate an adult Welsh Springer Spaniel. He will stand about 17–19 inches at the shoulder when fully grown, so choose a crate whose measurements will allow him to fully stand up, lie down and turn around.

BEDDING AND CRATE PADS

Your puppy will enjoy some type of soft bedding in his "room" (the crate), something he can snuggle into to feel cozy and secure. Old towels or blankets are good choices for a young pup, since he may (and probably will) have a toileting accident or two in the crate or decide to chew on the bedding material. Once he is fully

or good for your puppy, so use caution when you go puppy-toy shopping.

Welshies can be chewers, especially while teething. The best "chewcifiers" are nylon and hard rubber bones, which are safe to gnaw on and come in sizes appropriate for all age groups and breeds. Be especially careful of natural bones, which can splinter or develop dangerous sharp edges; pups can easily swallow or choke on those bone splinters. Veterinarians often tell of surgical nightmares involving bits of splintered bone, because in addition to the danger of choking, the sharp pieces can damage the intestinal tract.

Similarly, rawhide chews, while a favorite of most dogs and puppies, can be equally dangerous. Pieces of rawhide are easily swallowed after they get soft and gummy from chewing, and dogs have been known to choke on pieces of ingested rawhide.

Rawhide chews should be offered only when you can supervise the puppy.

Soft woolly toys are special puppy favorites. They come in a wide variety of cute shapes and sizes; some look like little stuffed animals. Puppies love to shake them up and toss them about or simply carry them around. Be careful of fuzzy toys that have button eyes or noses that your pup could chew off and swallow, and make sure that he does not disembowel a squeaky toy to remove the squeaker! Braided rope toys are similar in that they are fun to chew and toss around, but they shred easily and the strings are easy to swallow. The strings are not digestible and, if the puppy doesn't pass them in his stool, he could end up at the vet's office. As with rawhides, your puppy should be closely monitored with rope toys.

If you believe that your pup has ingested a piece of one of his

Enjoying the comforts of home, Fairwinds Fanny Bertha cuddles up. Puppies need to rest just as much as they need to play and explore.

Once your Welshie is house-trained, you can explore the wide range of dog beds available. Thomas (LEFT) and Kirby (RIGHT) are cozy in their plush beds.

TOYS 'R SAFE

The vast array of tantalizing puppy toys is staggering. Stroll through any pet shop or pet-supply outlet and you will see that the choices can be overwhelming. However, not all dog toys are safe or sensible. Most young puppies enjoy soft woolly toys that they can snuggle with and carry around. (You know they have outgrown them when they shred them up!) Avoid toys that have buttons, tabs or other enhancements that can be chewed off and swallowed. Soft toys that squeak are fun, but make sure your puppy does not disembowel the toy and remove (and swallow) the squeaker. Toys that rattle or make noise can excite a puppy, but they present the same danger as the squeaky kind and so require supervision. Hard rubber toys that bounce can also entertain a pup, but make sure that the toy is too big for your pup to swallow.

toys, check his stools for the next couple of days to see if he passes the item when he defecates. At the same time, also watch for signs of intestinal distress. A call to your veterinarian might be in order to get his advice and be on the safe side.

An all-time favorite toy for puppies (young and old!) is the empty gallon milk jug. Hard plastic juice containers—46 ounces or more—are also excellent. Such containers make lots of noise when they are batted about, and puppies go crazy with delight as they play with them. However, they don't often last very long, so be sure to remove and replace them when they get chewed up.

A word of caution about homemade toys: be careful with your choices of non-traditional play objects. Never use old shoes or socks, since a puppy cannot distinguish between the old ones on which he's allowed to chew and the new ones in your closet that are strictly off limits. That principle applies to anything that resembles something that you don't want your puppy to chew.

COLLARS

A lightweight nylon collar is the best choice for a very young pup. Quick-click collars are easy to put on and remove, and they can be adjusted as the puppy grows. Introduce him to his collar as soon as he comes home to get him accustomed to wearing it. He'll get used to it quickly and won't mind it a bit. Make sure that it is snug enough that it won't slip off, yet loose enough to be comfortable for the pup. You should be able to slip two fingers between the collar and his neck. Check the collar often, as puppies grow in spurts, and his collar can become too tight almost overnight.

LEASHES

A 6-foot nylon lead is an excellent choice for a young puppy. It is lightweight and not as tempting to chew as a leather lead. You can switch to a 6-foot leather lead after your pup has grown and is used to walking politely on a lead. For initial puppy walks and house-training purposes, you should invest in a shorter lead so that you have more control over the puppy. At first, you don't want him wandering too far away from you, and when taking him out for toileting you will want to keep

How do you make a Welshie smile? It looks like some time outdoors and a fun toy to play with will do the trick!

him in the specific area chosen for his potty spot.

Once the puppy is trained to heel with a traditional leash, you can consider purchasing a retractable lead. A retractable lead is excellent for walking adult dogs that are already leash-wise. This type of lead expands to allow the dog to roam farther away from you and explore a wider area when out walking, and also retracts when you need to keep him close to you.

HOME SAFETY FOR YOUR PUPPY

The importance of puppy-proofing cannot be overstated. In addition to making your house

---

COST OF OWNERSHIP

The purchase price of your puppy is merely the first expense in the typical dog budget. Quality dog food, veterinary care (sickness and health maintenance), dog supplies and grooming costs will add up to big bucks every year. Can you adequately afford to support a canine addition to the family?

A Dog-Safe Home

The dog-safety police are taking you on a house tour. Let's go room by room and see how safe your own home is for your new pup. The following items are doggy dangers, so either they must be removed or the dog should be monitored or not have access to these areas.

Living Room
- house plants (some varieties are poisonous)
- fireplace or wood-burning stove
- paint on the walls (lead-based paint is toxic)
- lead drapery weights (toxic lead)
- lamps and electrical cords
- carpet cleaners or deodorizers

Outdoor
- swimming pool
- pesticides
- toxic plants
- lawn fertilizers

Bathroom
- blue water in the toilet bowl
- medicine cabinet (filled with potentially deadly bottles)
- soap bars, bleach, drain cleaners, etc.
- tampons

Kitchen
- household cleaners in the kitchen cabinets
- glass jars and canisters
- sharp objects (like kitchen knives, scissors and forks)
- garbage can (with remnants of good-smelling things like onions, potato skins, apple or pear cores, peach pits, coffee beans, etc.)
- "people foods" that are toxic to dogs, like chocolate, raisins, grapes, nuts and onions

Garage
- antifreeze
- fertilizers (including rose foods)
- pesticides and rodenticides
- pool supplies (chlorine and other chemicals)
- oil and gasoline in containers
- sharp objects, electrical cords and power tools

comfortable for your Welsh Springer Spaniel's arrival, you also must make sure that your house is safe for your puppy before you bring him home. There are countless hazards in the owner's personal living environment that a pup can sniff, chew, swallow or destroy. Many are obvious; others are not. Do a thorough advance house check to remove or rearrange those things that could hurt your puppy, keeping any potentially dangerous items out of areas to which he will have access.

Electrical cords are especially dangerous, since puppies view them as irresistible chew toys. Unplug and remove all exposed cords or fasten them beneath baseboards where the puppy cannot reach them. Veterinarians and firefighters can tell you horror stories about electrical burns and house fires that resulted from puppy-chewed electrical cords. Consider this a most serious precaution for your puppy and the rest of your family.

Scout your home for tiny objects that might be seen at a pup's eye level. Keep medication bottles and cleaning supplies well out of reach, and do the same with waste baskets and other trash containers. It goes without saying that you should not use rodent poison or other toxic chemicals in any puppy

TOXIC PLANTS

Plants are natural puppy magnets, but many can be harmful, even fatal, if ingested by a puppy or adult dog. Scout your yard and home interior and remove any plants, bushes or flowers that could be even mildly dangerous. It could save your puppy's life. You can obtain a complete list of toxic plants from your veterinarian, at the public library or by looking online.

area and that you must keep such containers safely locked up. You will be amazed at how many places a curious puppy can discover!

Once your house has cleared inspection, check your yard. A sturdy fence, well embedded into the ground, will give your dog a safe place to play and potty. Welsh Springer Spaniels are athletic dogs, so a 6-foot-high fence should be considered necessary as a safety precaution to contain an agile youngster or adult. Check the fence periodically for necessary repairs. If there is a weak link or space to squeeze through, you can be sure a determined Welsh Springer Spaniel will discover it.

The garage and shed can be hazardous places for a pup, as things like fertilizers, chemicals and tools are usually kept there. It's best to keep these areas off limits to the pup. Antifreeze is especially dangerous to dogs, as they find the taste appealing and it takes only a few licks from the driveway to kill a dog, puppy or adult, small breed or large.

PUPPY SHOTS

Puppies are born with natural antibodies that protect them from most canine diseases. They receive more antibodies from the colostrum in their mother's milk. These immunities wear off, however, and must be replaced through a series of vaccines. Puppy shots are given at 3- to 4-week intervals starting at 6 to 8 weeks of age through 12 to 16 weeks of age. Booster shots are given after one year of age, and every one to three years thereafter, depending on the vaccine.

VISITING THE VETERINARIAN

A good veterinarian is your Welsh Springer Spaniel puppy's best health-insurance policy. If

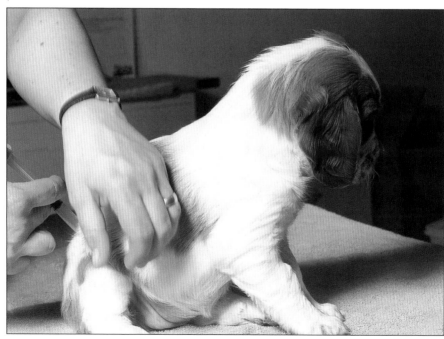

Having your puppy examined by the veterinarian and keeping current on the pup's vaccinations are absolute necessities.

you do not already have a vet, ask friends and experienced dog people in your area for recommendations so that you can select a vet before you bring your Welsh Springer Spaniel puppy home. Also arrange for your puppy's first veterinary examination beforehand, since many vets do not have appointments immediately available and your puppy should visit the vet within a day or so of coming home.

It's important to make sure that your puppy's first visit to the vet is a pleasant and positive one. The vet should take great care to befriend the pup and handle him gently to make their first meeting a positive experience. The vet will give the pup a thorough physical examination and set up a schedule for vaccinations and other necessary wellness visits. Be sure to show your vet any health and inoculation records, which you should have received from your breeder. Your vet is a great source of canine health information, so be sure to ask questions and take notes. Creating a health journal for your puppy will make a handy reference for his wellness and any future health problems that may arise.

MEETING THE FAMILY

Your Welsh Springer Spaniel's homecoming is an exciting time for all members of the family, and it's only natural that

THE FIRST FAMILY MEETING
Your puppy's first day at home should be quiet and uneventful. Despite his wagging tail, he is still wondering where his mom and siblings are! Let him make friends with other members of the family on his own terms; don't overwhelm him. You have a lifetime ahead to get to know each other!

everyone will be eager to meet him, pet him and play with him. However, for the puppy's sake, it's best to make these initial family meetings as uneventful as possible so that the pup is not overwhelmed with too much too soon. Remember, he has just left his dam and his littermates and is away from the breeder's home for the first time. Despite his fuzzy wagging tail, he is still apprehensive and wondering where he is and who all these strange humans are. It's best to let him explore on his own and meet the family members as he feels comfortable. Let him investigate all the new smells, sights and sounds at his own pace. Children should be especially careful to not get overly excited, use loud voices or hug the pup too tightly. Be calm, gentle and affectionate, and be ready to comfort him if he appears frightened or uneasy.

Be sure to show your puppy his new crate during this first

day home. Toss a treat or two inside the crate; if he associates the crate with food, he will associate the crate with good things. If he is comfortable with the crate, you can offer him his first

meal inside it. Leave the door ajar so he can wander in and out as he chooses.

FIRST NIGHT IN HIS NEW HOME

So much has happened in your Welsh Springer Spaniel puppy's first day away from the breeder. He's had his first car ride to his new home. He's met his new human family and perhaps the other family pets. He has explored his new house and yard, at least those places where he is to be allowed during his first weeks at home. He may have visited his new veterinarian. He has eaten his first meal or two away from his dam and littermates. Surely that's enough to tire out an eight-week-old Welsh Springer Spaniel pup...or so you hope!

It's bedtime. During the day, the pup investigated his crate, which is his new den and sleeping space, so it is not entirely strange to him. Line the crate with a soft towel or blanket that he can snuggle into and gently place him into the crate for the night. Some breeders send home a piece of bedding from where the pup slept with his littermates, and those familiar scents are a great comfort for the puppy on his first night without his siblings.

He will probably whine or cry. The puppy is objecting to the confinement and the fact that he is alone for the first time. This can

THE CRITICAL SOCIALIZATION PERIOD

Canine research has shown that a puppy's 8th through 20th week is the most critical learning period of his life. This is when the puppy "learns to learn," a time when he needs positive experiences to build confidence and stability. Puppies who are not exposed to different people and situations outside the home during this period can grow up to be fearful and sometimes aggressive. This is also the best time for puppy lessons, since he has not yet acquired any bad habits that could undermine his ability to learn.

be a stressful time for you as well as for the pup. It's important that you remain strong and don't let the puppy out of his crate to comfort him. He will fall asleep eventually. If you release him, the puppy will learn that crying means "out" and will continue that habit. You are laying the groundwork for future habits. Some breeders find that soft music can soothe a crying pup and help him get to sleep.

SOCIALIZING YOUR PUPPY

The first 20 weeks of your Welsh Springer Spaniel puppy's life are the most important of his entire lifetime. A properly socialized puppy will grow up to be a confident and stable adult who will be a pleasure to live with and a welcome addition to the neighborhood.

The importance of socialization cannot be overemphasized. Research on canine behavior has proven that puppies who are not exposed to new sights, sounds, people and animals during their first 20 weeks of life will grow up to be timid and fearful, even aggressive, and unable to flourish outside of their familiar home environment.

Socializing your puppy is not difficult and, in fact, will be a fun time for you both. Lead training goes hand in hand with socialization, so your puppy will be learning how to walk on a lead at the

same time that he's meeting the neighborhood. Because the Welsh Springer Spaniel is such a terrific breed, everyone will enjoy meeting "the new kid on the block." Take him for short walks to the park and to other dog-friendly places where he will encounter new people, especially children. Puppies automatically recognize children as "little people" and are drawn to play with them. Just make sure that you supervise these meetings and that the children do not get too rough or encourage him to play too hard. An overzealous pup can often nip too hard, frightening the child and in turn making the puppy overly excited. A bad experience in puppyhood can impact a dog for life, so a pup that has a negative experience with a child may grow up to be shy or even aggressive around children.

Springers at play! A Welshie pup enjoys some rough-and-tumble with an English Springer Spaniel playmate.

Your pup will be attentive to every new sight and sound in his environment.

Take your puppy along on your daily errands. Puppies are natural "people magnets," and most people who see your pup will want to pet him. All of these encounters will help to mold him into a confident adult dog. Likewise, you will soon feel like a confident, responsible dog owner, rightly proud of your mannerly Welsh Springer Spaniel. In addition to meeting humans, your puppy must also be socialized with other dogs. Luckily, Welshies are not dog-aggressive; in fact, they are very friendly, even exuberant, around other dogs.

Be especially careful of your puppy's encounters and experiences during the eight-to-ten-week-old period, which is also called the "fear period." This is a serious imprinting period, and all contact during this time should be gentle and positive. A frightening or negative event could leave a permanent impression that could affect his future behavior if a similar situation arises.

Also make sure that your puppy has received his first and second rounds of vaccinations before you expose him to other dogs or bring him to places that other dogs may frequent. Avoid dog parks and other strange-dog areas until your vet assures you that your puppy is fully immunized and resistant to the diseases that can be passed between canines. Discuss safe early socialization with your breeder and vet, as some recommend socializing the puppy even before he has received all of his inoculations, depending on the puppy.

LEADER OF THE PUPPY'S PACK
Like other canines, your puppy needs an authority figure, someone he can look up to and regard as the leader of his "pack." His first pack leader was his dam, who taught him to be polite and not chew too hard on her ears or nip at her muzzle. He learned those same lessons from his littermates. If he played too rough, they cried in pain and stopped the game, which sent an important message to the rowdy puppy.

As puppies play together, they are also struggling to determine who will be the boss. Being pack animals, dogs need someone to be in charge. If a litter of puppies

remained together beyond puppy-hood, one of the pups would emerge as the strongest one, the one who calls the shots.

Once your puppy leaves the pack, he will look intuitively for a new leader. If he does not recognize you as that leader, he will try to assume that position for himself. Of course, it is hard to imagine your adorable Welsh Springer Spaniel puppy trying to be in charge when he is so small and seemingly helpless. You must remember that these are natural canine instincts. Do not cave in and allow your pup to get the upper "paw"!

Just as socialization is so important during these first 20 weeks, so too is your puppy's early education. He was born without any bad habits. He does not know what is good or bad behavior. If he does things like nipping and digging, it's because he is having fun and doesn't know that humans consider these things as "bad." It's your job to teach him proper puppy manners, and this is the best time to accomplish that—before he has developed bad habits, since it is much more difficult to "unlearn" or correct unacceptable learned behavior than to teach good behavior from the start.

Make sure that all members of the family understand the importance of being consistent when training their new puppy. If you tell the puppy to stay off

A puppy's dam is often looked at as leader of the pack, which is the role you will assume in your Welshie pup's new life.

the sofa and your daughter allows him to cuddle on the couch to watch her favorite television show, your pup will be confused about what he is and is not allowed to do. Have a family conference before your pup comes home so that everyone understands the basic principles of puppy training and the rules you have set forth for the pup, and agrees to follow them.

The old saying that "an ounce of prevention is worth a pound of cure" is especially true when it comes to puppies. It is much easier to prevent inappropriate behavior than it is to change it. It's also easier and less stressful for the pup, since it will keep discipline to a minimum and create a more positive learning environment for him. That, in turn, will also be easier on you!

Here are a few commonsense tips to keep your belongings safe and your puppy out of trouble:
- Keep your closet doors closed and your shoes, socks and other apparel off the floor so your puppy can't get at them.
- Keep a secure lid on the trash container or put the trash where your puppy can't dig into it. He can't damage what he can't reach!
- Supervise your puppy at all times to make sure he is not getting into mischief. If he starts to chew the corner of the rug, you can distract him instantly by tossing a toy for him to fetch. You also will be able to whisk him outside when you notice that he is about to piddle on the carpet. If you can't see your puppy, you can't teach him or correct his behavior.

SOLVING PUPPY PROBLEMS

CHEWING AND NIPPING
Nipping at fingers and toes is normal puppy behavior. Chewing is also the way that puppies investigate their surroundings. However, you will have to teach your puppy that chewing anything other than his toys is not acceptable. That won't happen overnight and at times puppy teeth will test your patience. However, if you allow nipping and chewing to

continue, just think about the damage that a mature Welsh Springer Spaniel can do with a full set of adult teeth.

Whenever your puppy nips your hand or fingers, cry out "Ouch!" in a loud voice, which should startle your puppy and stop him from nipping, even if only for a moment. Immediately distract him by offering a small treat or an appropriate toy for him to chew instead (which means having chew toys and puppy treats handy or in your pockets at all times). Praise him when he takes the toy and tell him what a good fellow he is. Praise is just as or even more important in puppy training as discipline and correction.

Puppies also tend to nip at children more often than adults,

TEETHING TIME

All puppies chew. It's normal canine behavior. Chewing just plain feels good to a puppy, especially during the three- to five-month teething period when the adult teeth are breaking through the gums. Rather than attempting to eliminate such a strong natural chewing instinct, you will be more successful if you redirect it and teach your puppy what he may or may not chew. Correct inappropriate chewing with a sharp "No!" and offer him a chew toy, praising him when he takes it. Don't become discouraged. Chewing usually decreases after the adult teeth have come in.

since they perceive little ones to be more vulnerable and more similar to their littermates. Teach your children appropriate responses to nipping behavior. If they are unable to handle it themselves, you may have to intervene. Puppy nips can be quite painful and a child's frightened reaction will only encourage a puppy to nip harder, which is a natural canine response. As with all other puppy situations, interaction between your Welsh Springer Spaniel puppy and children should be supervised.

Chewing on objects, not just family members' fingers and ankles, is also normal canine behavior that can be especially tedious (for the owner, not the pup) during the teething period when the puppy's adult teeth are coming in. At this stage, chewing just plain feels good. Furniture legs and cabinet corners are common puppy favorites. Shoes and other personal items also taste pretty good to a pup.

To discourage improper chewing, be sure to provide plenty of safe chew toys and praise your dog for using them.

The best solution is, once again, prevention. If you value something, keep it tucked away and out of reach. You can't hide your dining-room table in a closet, but you can try to deflect the chewing by applying a bitter product made just to deter dogs from chewing. This spray-on substance is vile-tasting, although safe for dogs, and most puppies will avoid the forbidden object after one tiny taste. You also can apply the product to your leather leash if the puppy tries to chew on his lead during leash-training sessions.

Keep a ready supply of safe chews handy to offer your Welsh Springer Spaniel as a distraction when he starts to chew on something that's a "no-no." Remember, at this tender age he does not yet know what is permitted or forbidden, so you have to be "on call" every minute he's awake and on the prowl.

You may lose a treasure or two during puppy's growing-up period, and the furniture could sustain a nasty nick or two. These can be trying times, so be prepared for those inevitable accidents and comfort yourself in knowing that this too shall pass.

JUMPING UP

Although Welsh Springer Spaniel pups are not known to be notorious jumpers, they are still puppies after all, and puppies jump up—on you, your guests, your counters and your furniture. Just another normal part of growing up, and one you need to meet head-on before it becomes an ingrained habit.

The key to jump correction is consistency. You cannot correct your Welsh Springer Spaniel for jumping up on you today, then allow it to happen tomorrow by greeting him with hugs and kisses. As you have learned by now, consistency is critical to all puppy lessons.

For starters, try turning your back as soon as the puppy jumps. Jumping up is a means of gaining your attention and, if the pup can't see your face, he may get discouraged and learn that he loses eye contact with his beloved master when he jumps up.

DIGGING OUT

Some dogs love to dig. Others wouldn't think of it. Digging is considered "self-rewarding behavior" because it's fun! Of all the digging solutions offered by the experts, most are only marginally successful and none are guaranteed to work. The best cure is prevention, which means removing the dog from the offending site when he digs as well as distracting him when you catch him digging so that he turns his attentions elsewhere. That means that you have to supervise your dog's yard time. An unsupervised digger can create havoc with your landscaping or, worse, run away!

Leash corrections also work, and most puppies respond well to a leash tug if they jump. Grasp the leash close to the puppy's collar and give a quick tug downward, using the command "Off." Do not use the word "Down," since "Down" is used to teach the puppy to lie down, which is a separate action that he will learn during his education in the basic commands. As soon as the puppy has backed off, tell him to sit and immediately praise him for doing so. This will take many repetitions and won't be accomplished quickly, so don't get discouraged or give up; you must be even more persistent than your puppy.

Another method used for jump correction is the spritzer bottle. Fill a spray bottle with water mixed with a bit of lemon juice or vinegar. As soon as puppy jumps, command him "Off" and spritz him with the water mixture. Of course, that means having the spray bottle handy whenever or wherever jumping usually happens.

Yet another method to discourage jumping is grasping the puppy's paws and holding them gently but firmly until he struggles to get away. Wait a brief moment or two, then release his paws and give him a command to sit. He should eventually learn that jumping gets him into an uncomfortable predicament.

CONFINEMENT

It is wise to keep your puppy confined to a small "puppy-proofed" area of the house for his first few weeks at home. Gate or block off a space near the door he will use for outdoor potty trips. Expandable baby gates are useful to create your puppy's designated area. If he is allowed to roam through the entire house or even only several rooms, it will be more difficult to house-train him.

Children are major victims of puppy jumping, since puppies view little people as ready targets for jumping up as well as nipping. If your children (or their friends) are unable to dispense jump corrections, you will have to intervene and handle it for them.

Important to prevention is also knowing what you should not do. Never kick your Welsh Springer Spaniel (for any reason, not just for jumping) or knock him in the chest with your knee. That maneuver could actually harm your puppy very badly.

PUPPY WHINING

Puppies often cry and whine, just as infants and little children do. It's their way of telling us that they are lonely or in need of attention. Your puppy will miss his litter-mates and will feel insecure when he is left alone. You may be out of the house or just in another room, but he will still feel alone. During these times, the puppy's crate should be his personal comfort station, a place all his own where he can feel safe and secure. Once he learns that being alone is okay and not something to be feared, he will settle down without crying or objecting. You might want to leave a radio on while he is crated, as the sound of human voices can be soothing and will give the impression that people are around.

Give your puppy a favorite cuddly toy or chew toy to entertain him whenever he is crated. You will both be happier: the puppy because he is safe in his den and you because he is quiet, safe and not getting into puppy escapades that can wreak havoc in your house or cause him danger.

To make sure that your puppy will always view his crate as a safe and cozy place, never, ever use the crate as punishment. That's the best way to turn the crate into a negative place that the pup will want to avoid. Sure, you can use the crate for your own peace of mind if your puppy is getting into trouble and needs some "time out." Just don't let him know that! Never scold the pup and immediately place him into the crate. Count to ten, give him a couple of hugs and maybe a treat, then scoot him into his crate.

It's also important not to make a big fuss when he is released from the crate. That will make getting out of the crate more appealing than being in the crate, which is just the opposite of what you are trying to achieve.

THE FAMILY FELINE

A resident cat has feline squatter's rights. The cat will treat the newcomer (your puppy) as she sees fit, regardless of what you do or say, so it's best to let the two of them work things out on their own terms. Cats have a height advantage and will generally leap to higher ground to avoid direct contact with a rambunctious pup. Some will hiss and boldly swat at a pup who passes by or tries to reach the cat. Keep the puppy under control in the presence of the cat and they will eventually become accustomed to each other.

Here's a hint: move the cat's litter box where the puppy can't get into it! It's best to do so well before the pup comes home so the cat is used to the new location.

WELSH SPRINGER SPANIEL

FEEDING

The health of your dog has a lot to do with what you feed him. Therefore it is of the utmost importance to select the food that suits him best. Factors to be considered are his age, his condition and his activity level: is he a puppy or an adult; is he too thin or too fat; and is he an active working or competition dog or a pet with a quieter lifestyle?

Although there are dozens of brands, there are a few basic types of dog food: dry food, semi-moist food and canned food. Dry foods are the most common, and some owners will mix some canned or semi-moist food in with the dry or perhaps mix in some fresh meat, like chicken. Although some "people" foods, like chocolate, onions, nuts, raisins, grapes and quantities of garlic, are toxic to dogs and should not be given to your Welshie, most dogs will enjoy treats like green beans, a piece of apple or even lettuce. Do not offer your Welshie any food that is oily or spicy.

When selecting your dog's diet, three stages of development must be considered: the puppy stage, the adult stage and the senior stage. Further, your puppy gets important nutrition before he comes home with you.

NURSING AND WEANING

A most moving and wondrous sight occurs when the newborn puppy, still wet, blind, deaf and unable to walk, knows within minutes to find his way to his mother's teats. The time a breeder cherishes is when the litter has been born and all of the puppies

NOT HUNGRY?

No dog in his right mind would turn down his dinner, would he? If you notice that your dog has lost interest in his food, there could be any number of causes. Dental problems are a common cause of appetite loss, one that is often overlooked. If your dog has a toothache, a loose tooth or sore gums from infection, chances are it doesn't feel so good to chew. Think about when you've had a toothache! If your dog does not approach the food bowl with his usual enthusiasm, look inside his mouth for signs of a problem. Whatever the cause, you'll want to consult your vet so that your chow hound can get back to his happy, hungry self as soon as possible.

A litter of seven will certainly keep a mother busy! The pups are getting proper nutrition from their mother's milk.

are suckling enthusiastically from their tired but very contented mom, who is still busy cleaning and drying them. Those first moments of drinking are very important, because this early milk contains colostrum, which helps to protect the puppies during the first five to six weeks of their lives. Although there are many excellent milk products available, there is nothing as good as mother's milk. Should the mother for some reason not have sufficient milk or be unable to feed the pups, it is of the utmost importance that the breeder seeks the help of his vet to advise him what quality and quantity of milk to feed the puppies. Hand feeding

puppies is a lot of work. Not only do the puppies have to be fed every two hours around the clock, but they need to be massaged after each feeding to stimulate their digestion and to have them produce stools.

Depending on the size of the litter and the quantity of milk that the mother has, weaning starts at two to three weeks, usually beginning with small portions of suitable solid food. Most breeders like to start with minced meat and a couple of days later with some milky food. Gradually the quantities and the number of meals are increased until the pups are six weeks old. Selection of the most suitable good-quality diet at this time is essential, for a puppy's fastest growth rate is during the first year of life. Veterinarians or experienced breeders will be able to offer you good advice in this regard.

PUPPY DIETS

Puppy and junior diets should be well balanced for the needs of your dog so that except in certain circumstances additional vitamins,

SWITCHING FOODS

There are certain times in a dog's life when it becomes necessary to switch his food; for example, from puppy to adult food and then from adult to senior-dog food. Additionally, you may decide to feed your pup a different type of food from what he received from the breeder, and there may be "emergency" situations in which you can't find your dog's normal brand and have to offer something else temporarily. Anytime a change is made, for whatever reason, the switch must be done gradually. You don't want to upset the dog's stomach or end up with a picky eater who refuses to eat something new. A tried-and-true approach is, over the course of about a week, to mix a little of the new food in with the old, increasing the proportion of new to old as the days progress. At the end of the week, you'll be feeding his regular portions of the new food, and he will barely notice the change.

minerals and proteins will not be required.

When you decided to buy your puppy, the breeder probably instructed you on how to feed the puppy once you brought him home. If he didn't, ask him. This is important for two reasons. First, coming to live in totally new surroundings with so many new experiences is already a stressful experience for the puppy, so a continuation of his diet will help him adjust. His tummy may be upset the first couple of days, or he may even refuse to eat for a day or two, but don't worry about that. As soon as he is settled, he will eat again, especially if it's the food that he is used to. Second, the breeder most likely has a lot of experience in feeding mature dogs and puppies and keeping them in a peak condition, so it would be wise to listen to his advice. Most breeders will provide you with an exact list of what to feed the

Young Welshies can sometimes be picky eaters, but it's a phase they will outgrow.

DIET DON'TS

- Got milk? Don't give it to your dog! Dogs cannot tolerate large quantities of cows' milk, as they do not have the enzymes to digest lactose.
- You may have heard of dog owners who add raw eggs to their dogs' food for a shiny coat or to make the food more palatable, but consumption of raw eggs too often can cause a deficiency of the vitamin biotin.
- Avoid feeding table scraps, as they will upset the balance of the dog's complete food. Additionally, fatty or highly seasoned foods can cause upset canine stomachs.
- Do not offer raw meat to your dog. Raw meat can contain parasites; it also is high in fat.
- Vitamin A toxicity in dogs can be caused by too much liver, especially if the dog already gets enough vitamin A in his balanced diet, which should be the case.
- Bones like chicken, pork chop and other soft bones are not suitable, as they easily splinter.

puppy at each stage of his life, and we strongly advise you to follow these instructions. Once your puppy is a mature one- or two-year-old, you can change his diet to what is more convenient for you (availability, costs, etc.) but, with the growing puppy and youngster, stick to the breeder's diet. And remember that if ten breeders are discussing the feeding of their dogs, you will hear ten different opinions, and all of them will be right!

Your puppy will need three or four meals a day until he is about nine months old; then you can cut back to two daily meals. Some people prefer to feed the adult dog once a day, but if your dog loves his food, he probably won't go along with that! He might prefer to have a breakfast and a dinner. It also is healthier for a dog's digestion to eat two smaller meals a day than one large daily portion.

Sometimes a Welsh Springer can be a finicky eater. Don't make the mistake in trying to find out what he would like to eat, because that will most certainly worsen the problem. Give him the food you want him to eat and if he doesn't eat it, take it away. Let him be hungry for a few hours and you will find that next time you feed him, he will approach his food bowl with more enthusiasm. It is important, though, that when he is eating poorly, the food he does eat is of the highest quality. Welshies can be poor eaters until they are 18 to 24 months old, and as a result be thin for some time. Don't despair—your Welshie will eat and within a couple of years you have to be careful that he is not growing too fat!

Adult Diets

A dog is considered an adult when he has stopped growing. The growth is in height and/or length. Do not consider the dog's weight when the decision is made to switch from a puppy diet to an adult-maintenance diet. Again you should rely on your breeder's advice. A Welsh Springer Spaniel generally reaches adulthood between two-and-a-half to three-and-a-half years of age, though some dogs are fully mature at two years old while others look their best when they are four.

Whatever you are going to feed your dog, don't rely entirely on the quantities given in the manufacturer's instructions. Every dog has different requirements, as in humans. Where one dog will grow fat on a smaller portion, another will need double the quantity. So it is best to "feed with your eyes."

Factor treats into your dog's overall daily caloric intake, and avoid offering table scraps, as this can encourage begging, cause an upset tummy and lead to overfeeding. Overweight dogs are more prone to health problems. Research has even shown that

obesity takes years off a dog's life. With that in mind, resist the urge to overfeed and over-treat. Don't make unnecessary additions to your dog's diet, whether with tidbits or with extra vitamins and minerals unless advised by your vet.

The amount of food needed for proper maintenance will vary depending on the individual dog's activity level, but you will be able to tell whether the daily portions are keeping him in good shape. With the wide variety of good complete foods available, choosing what to feed your adult Welshie is largely a matter of personal preference. Just as with the puppy, the adult dog should have consistency in his mealtimes and feeding

Healthy adult Welshies normally are eager eaters. If your dog seems uninterested in his food, something could be wrong.

When you see gray on the muzzle, you know your Welshie is getting older. Consult your vet about possible dietary changes for your senior dog.

a higher-protein or senior-formu-lated food or whether your current adult-dog food contains sufficient nutrition for the senior. Depending on the condition of the dog and the food he currently eats, the vet may or may not recommend a change.

Watching the dog's weight remains essential, even more so in the senior stage. Here again, "feed with your eyes." Older dogs are

place. In addition to a consistent routine, regular mealtimes also allow the owner to see how much his dog is eating. If the dog seems never to be satisfied or, likewise, becomes uninterested in his food, the owner will know right away that something is wrong and can consult the vet.

DIETS FOR THE AGING DOG

What does aging have to do with your dog's diet? No, he won't get a discount at the local diner's early-bird special. Yes, he will require some dietary changes to accom-modate the changes that come along with increased age. One change is that the older dog's dietary needs become more simi-lar to that of a puppy. Specifically, dogs can metabolize more protein as youngsters and seniors than in the adult-maintenance stage. When your Welshie is around eight years old, discuss with your vet whether you need to switch to

THE BOVINE CANINE

Does your dog's grazing in the back yard have you wondering whether he's actually a farm animal in disguise? Many owners have noticed their dogs eating grass and wonder why! It is thought that dogs might eat grass to settle their stomachs or to relieve upset tummies. Even cats have been known to eat grass for the same reasons! Stomach upset can be caused by various things, including poor digestion and parasites.

Unfortunately, while the grass may make the dog feel better very temporarily, often they vomit shortly after eating it, as grass can be irritating to a dog's stomach lining. Even worse, who knows what he is ingesting along with the grass? He could be swallowing insects, germs or parasites, thus perpetuating the problem. Grass-eating should be discouraged when you catch the dog in the act, and a trip to the vet to determine the underlying cause is in order.

already more vulnerable to illness, and obesity only contributes to their susceptibility to problems. As the older dog becomes less active and thus exercises less, his regular portions may cause him to gain weight. At this point, you may consider decreasing his daily food intake or switching to a reduced-calorie food. As with other changes, you should consult your vet for advice.

As your dog gets older, few of his organs function up to par. The kidneys slow down and the intestines become less efficient. These age-related factors are often handled with a change in diet and a change in feeding schedule to

give smaller portions that are more easily digested. There is no single best diet for every older dog; it is up to you and your vet to find out which diet suits your senior Welshie best.

Bring water along when you go places with your dog. Every dog will need to cool down after a vigorous romp at the dog park.

QUENCHING HIS THIRST

Is your dog drinking more than normal and trying to lap up everything in sight? Excessive drinking has many different causes. Obvious causes for a dog's being thirstier than usual are hot weather and vigorous exercise. However, if your dog is drinking more for no apparent reason, you could have cause for concern. Serious conditions like kidney or liver disease, diabetes and various types of hormonal problems can all be indicated by excessive drinking. If you notice your dog's being excessively thirsty, contact your vet at once. Hopefully there will be a simpler explanation, but the earlier a serious problem is detected, the sooner it can be treated, with a better rate of cure.

DON'T FORGET THE WATER!

For a dog, it's always time for a drink! Regardless of what type of food he eats, there's no doubt that he needs plenty of water. Fresh cold water, in a clean bowl, should be available to your dog at all times. There are special circumstances, such as during puppy housebreaking, when you will want to monitor your pup's water intake so that you will be able to predict when he will need to relieve himself, but water must be available to him nonetheless. Water is essential for hydration and proper body function just as it is in humans.

You will get to know how much your dog typically drinks in a day. Of course, in the heat or if

Here I come! A
Welsh Springer
will not need
much
encouragement
to run off
some of his
sporting-dog
energy.

exercising vigorously, he will be more thirsty and will drink more. However, if he begins to drink noticeably more water for no apparent reason, this could signal any of various problems, and you are advised to consult your vet.

Water is the best drink for dogs. Some owners are tempted to give milk from time to time or to moisten dry food with milk, but dogs do not have the enzymes necessary to digest the lactose in milk, which is much different from the milk that nursing puppies receive. Therefore stick with clean fresh water to quench your dog's thirst, and always have it readily available to him.

You will find that your Welsh Springer Spaniel is a very sloppy drinker; he loves his water bowl and in his enthusiasm he will often put not only his mouth but

also both front paws in the bowl. Or he will take one last mouthful of water and before swallowing it come to you to tell you how much he loves you! A special spaniel bowl may help you keep the kitchen floor clean by keeping the dog's ears from getting in the water and dripping all over.

EXERCISE

All dogs require some form of exercise, regardless of breed. A sedentary lifestyle is as harmful to a dog as it is to a person. The Welsh Springer Spaniel is a very lively and active breed that requires a lot of free exercise. He might like to come with you on a shopping expedition but what he needs is to run around free, preferably in exciting surroundings, like woods or fields, where he can develop his hunting instincts. That being said, you can understand the importance of your Welshie's being taught to come to you reliably when called.

Owners often make mistakes in the exercise they give their dog. As the new puppy is an exciting thing, they often tend to give him too much exercise. It is only human to show off something you are very proud of, but it means that the small puppy is taken on too many walks. For a puppy up to six months, the yard is big enough. Take him to the park once a day to let him socialize and play with the other dogs for about 15 minutes. Once the puppy is about nine months old, you can extend the daily walks to an hour daily, and once he is a year old, his energy will be boundless.

We cannot stress the importance of exercise enough. It is essential to keep the dog's body fit, but it is also essential to his mental well-being. A bored dog will find something to do, which often manifests itself in some type of destructive behavior. In this sense, it is essential for your mental well-being too!

GROOMING

By grooming, we mean keeping a dog clean and tidy for his overall health, comfort and appearance. The coat of a Welsh Springer Spaniel is naturally straight, flat and soft to the touch, never wiry or wavy. It is sufficiently dense to be waterproof, thornproof and weatherproof. The back of the forelegs, the hindlegs above the hocks, the chest and the underside of the body are moderately feathered. The ears and tail are lightly feathered. The color is a rich red and white; any pattern is acceptable and any white area may be flecked with red ticking.

You will find that this coat doesn't need much care as long as the dog is healthy and is brushed and combed regularly, at least once a week but preferably more often. Because of the silky texture of the coat, the hairs can easily form

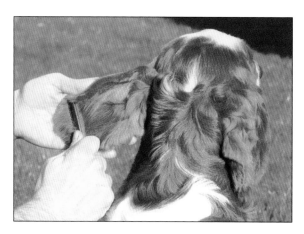

tangles and mats but a thorough combing session will prevent that. Don't worry when after a walk in bad weather your whiter-than-white Welshie comes home all muddy and dirty. After a bath and a good rub with a towel, you'll find that he dries off in a warm room and the white is pearly white again. You will find that there really is no need to bathe him often.

BRUSHING

Brushing should ideally be done every day. It takes little time, but the daily attention is important for health reasons and, when you start with a puppy, for reasons of bonding with your dog and establishing control. Future show dogs need to become used to being examined and standing still, and the daily brushing sessions will help.

Daily brushing is effective for removing dead hair and stimulating the dog's natural oils to add

The pet Welshie's coat does not need much special care beyond regular brushing and combing and a little trimming to keep him looking tidy.

Excess hair on the ears can easily be removed with the finger-and-thumb method, using rubber "thumblettes" to grip the hair.

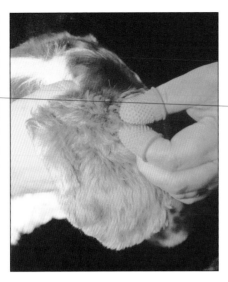

For brushing, you can use a natural medium-hard bristle brush, a glove with a bristle brush or a slicker brush, but be careful with a slicker brush, because you can easily hurt his skin. You need a comb for his ears and feathers and for overall removal of dead hair.

shine and a healthy look to the coat. The combing is necessary to prevent tangles from forming in such places as the armpits, behind the ears and in the feathers. At the same time you can check his ears, eyes and paws for cuts, thorns or any sign of infection.

TRIMMING

The coat needs trimming, just once every three or four months. The coat on a Welshie's body and head will stay flat and straight but his ears, throat, tail and feet will need trimming. You can always ask the breeder for help, and it is highly recommended and very rewarding if you learn to trim your dog yourself.

Although he doesn't grow much coat the first seven or eight months of his life, the hair on his feet will grow rather quickly. If you remove this superfluous hair, he will not only look tidier but also will get used to having his feet trimmed at an early age. Untrimmed feet not only look untidy but can also be uncomfortable for the dog and bring a lot of dirt into the house. Trim the hair away between the pads on the undersides of the feet—cut level with the pads. Trim the hair between the toes; pull up the hair between the toes and cut downwards, and then cut around the feet.

The hair on the throat is trimmed with thinning shears.

Excess hair on the ears can be removed fairly easily from the ears by using a comb and pulling with your finger and thumb (you can use a surgical glove to have a better grip) or a trimming knife, the one with teeth (not with a razor blade in it). The hair on the edges can be removed by using thinning scissors. If you hold the ear near the edge with one hand and cut with the other, you will never cut in the dog's ear, which is very sensitive and can bleed profusely if cut. Use thinning scissors to cut the hair behind and below the ears, around the ear opening and on the inside of the earflap.

The throat is trimmed as far down as the breastbone with thinning scissors. The feathering on the hocks is trimmed with thinning scissors. Superfluous hair on the body should always be pulled out with your finger and thumb. This sometimes can be a laborious and time-consuming process; however, if you cut corners and use clippers or scissors, you will find that you have spoiled his silky and flat coat forever.

Be prepared, though: no matter how often you brush and trim your Welsh Springer, he will shed his hair and you will always find white hairs in the house. You will have to either get used to it or teach him right from the start not to sit on your chair or lie in your bed!

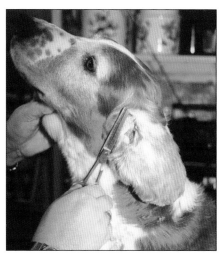

Thinning shears are also used on the inside of the ear.

BATHING

Dogs do not need to be bathed as often as humans, but sometimes a bath will be necessary. It is therefore important that you accustom your pup to being bathed as a puppy so that he is used to it when he grows up. You will have

Trim the hair between the footpads to keep the feet looking neat and to avoid irritation from excess hair.

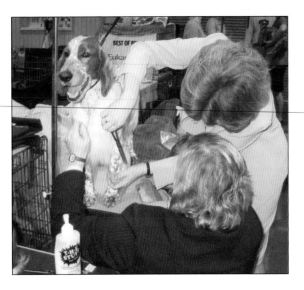

hair. Wash the head last; you do not want shampoo to drip into the dog's eyes while you are washing the rest of his body. Work the shampoo all the way down to the skin. You can use this opportunity to check the skin for any bumps, bites or other abnormalities. Do not neglect any area of the body—get all of the hard-to-reach places.

Once the dog has been thoroughly shampooed, he requires an equally thorough rinsing. Shampoo left in the coat can be irritating to the skin. Protect his

Show Welshies need more extensive grooming than dogs kept solely as pets. Here Ch. Gingerwood Recount Ruckus prepares for the ring with the help of one of his owners, Anne Gilliam, and Beth Holmes.

to bathe your dog the day before a show, and most owners like to bathe their bitches after they have been in season.

Before you are going to bathe your dog, comb through his coat thoroughly to remove any tangles. Make sure that your dog has a good non-slip surface to stand on. Begin by wetting the dog's coat. A shower or hose attachment is necessary for thoroughly wetting and rinsing the coat. Check the water temperature to make sure that it is neither too hot nor too cold. Put cotton balls in your Welshie's ears so that there is no chance of water or soap getting into the ear canals.

Next, apply shampoo to the dog's coat and work it into a good lather. You should purchase a shampoo that is made for dogs; do not use a product made for human

WATER SHORTAGE

No matter how well behaved your dog is, bathing is always a project! Nothing can substitute for a good warm bath, but owners do have the option of giving their dogs "dry" baths. Pet shops sell excellent products, in both powder and spray forms, designed for spot-cleaning your dog. These dry shampoos are convenient for touch-up jobs when you don't have the time to bathe your dog in the traditional way.

Muddy feet, messy behinds and smelly coats can be spot-cleaned and deodorized with a "wet-nap"-style cleaner. On those days when your dog insists on rolling in fresh goose droppings and there's no time for a bath, a spot bath can save the day. These pre-moistened wipes are also handy for other grooming needs like wiping faces, ears and eyes and freshening tails and behinds.

eyes from the shampoo by shielding them with your hand and directing the flow of water in the opposite direction.

At the end of the bath, be prepared for your dog to shake out his coat—you might want to stand back, but make sure you have a hold on the dog to keep him from running through the house. Have several absorbent towels on hand to dry him off.

EAR CLEANING

The ears should be kept clean and any excess hair inside the ear should be trimmed or gently plucked out. Ears can be cleaned with an ear cleaner made especially for dogs. Be on the lookout

Ears can be kept clean with an ear cleaner made especially for dogs and a soft cotton wipe. Be careful not to probe into the ear; clean only what you can see.

for any signs of infections or ear-mite infestation such as a foul odor or dark brown residue. During the summer look for grass seeds that may be picked up and can find their way into the ear canal. If your Welsh Springer Spaniel has been shaking his head or scratching at his ears frequently,

PRESERVING THOSE PEARLY WHITES

What do you treasure more than the smile of your beloved canine pal? Brushing your dog's teeth is just as important as brushing your own. Neglecting your dog's teeth can lead to tooth loss, periodontal disease and inflamed gums, not to mention bad breath. Can you find the time to brush your dog's teeth every day? If not, you should do so once a week at the very least, though every day is truly the ideal. Your vet should give your dog a thorough dental examination during his annual check-ups. A dental scraping, as shown in the picture, may also be done by the vet if needed.

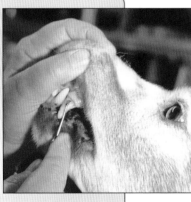

Pet shops sell terrific tooth-care devices, including specially designed toothbrushes, yummy toothpastes and finger-model brushes. You can use a human toothbrush with soft bristles, but never use human toothpastes, which can damage the dog's enamel. Baking soda is an alternative to doggie toothpastes, but your dog will be more receptive to canine toothpastes with the flavor of liver or hamburger. Make tooth care fun for your dog. Let him think that you're "horsing around" with his mouth. When brushing the dog's teeth, begin with the largest teeth (the canines) and proceed back toward the molars.

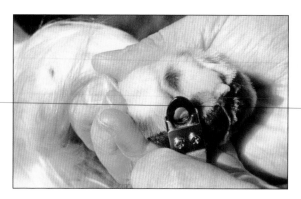

Your pet shop will have special clippers for trimming your Welshie's nails. Shown here are the popular guillotine-style clippers.

you will need to accustom your puppy to the procedure at a young age so that he will sit still (well, as still as he can) for his pedicures. Long nails can cause the dog's feet to spread, which is not good for him; likewise, long nails can hurt if they unintentionally scratch, not good for you!

Some dogs' nails are worn down naturally by regular walking on hard surfaces, so the frequency with which you clip depends on your individual dog. Look at his nails from time to time and clip as needed; a good way to know when it's time for a trim is if you hear your dog clicking as he walks across the floor.

this usually indicates a problem. Don't try to deal with this yourself. If you poke into the ear canal, you'll only succeed in aggravating things and can injure your dog. Contact your vet before the condition gets serious.

If you check your spaniel's ears regularly and use the ear cleaner when the ears don't look 100% clean, you will find that the spaniel's reputation for ear trouble is totally unfounded.

NAIL CLIPPING

Having their nails trimmed is not on many dogs' lists of favorite things to do. With this in mind,

There are several types of nail clippers and even electric nail-grinding tools made for dogs; first we'll discuss using the clipper. To start, have your clipper ready and some doggie treats on hand. You want your pup to view his nail-clipping sessions in a positive light, and what better way to convince him than with food? You may want to enlist the help of an assistant to comfort the pup and offer treats as you concentrate on the clipping itself. The guillotine-type clipper is thought of by many as the easiest type to use; the nail tip is inserted into the opening, and blades on the top and bottom snip it off in one clip.

Start by grasping the pup's paw; a little pressure on the foot pad causes the nail to extend,

Before and after: (LEFT) an untrimmed foot and (RIGHT) a trimmed foot.

making it easier to clip. Clip off a little at a time. If you can see the "quick," which is a blood vessel that runs through each nail, you will know how much to trim, as you do not want to cut into the quick. On that note, if you do cut the quick, which will cause bleeding, you can stem the flow of blood with a styptic pencil or other clotting agent. If you mistakenly nip the quick, do not panic or fuss, as this will cause the pup to be afraid. Simply reassure the

SCOOTING HIS BOTTOM

Here's a doggy problem that many owners tend to neglect. If your dog is scooting his rear end around the carpet, he probably is experiencing anal-sac impaction or blockage. The anal sacs are the two grape-sized glands on either side of the dog's anus. The dog cannot empty these glands, which become filled with a foul-smelling material. The dog may attempt to lick the area to relieve the pressure. He may also rub his anus on your walls, furniture or floors.

Don't neglect your dog's rear end during grooming sessions. By squeezing both sides of the anus with a soft cloth, you can express some of the material in the sacs. If the material is pasty and thick, you likely will need the assistance of a veterinarian. Vets know how to express the glands and can show you how to do it correctly without hurting the dog or spraying yourself with the unpleasant liquid.

pup, stop the bleeding and move on to the next nail. Don't be discouraged; you will become a professional canine pedicurist with practice.

You may or may not be able to see the quick, so it's best to just clip off a small bit at a time. If you see a dark dot in the center of the nail, this is the quick and your cue to stop clipping. Tell the puppy he's a "good boy" and offer a piece of treat with each nail. You can also use nail-clipping time to examine the footpads, making sure that they are not dry and cracked and that nothing has become embedded in them.

The nail grinder, the other choice, is many owners' first choice. Accustoming the puppy to the sound of the grinder and sensation of the buzz presents fewer challenges than the clipper, and there's no chance of cutting through the quick. Use the grinder on a low setting and always talk soothingly to your dog. He won't mind his salon visit, and he'll have nicely polished nails as well.

IDENTIFICATION AND TRAVEL

ID FOR YOUR DOG
You love your Welsh Springer Spaniel and want to keep him safe. Of course you take every precaution to prevent his escaping from the yard or becoming lost or stolen. You have a sturdy high fence and you always keep

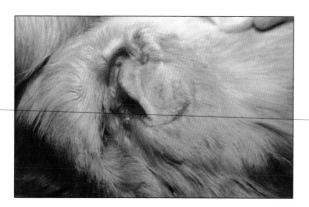

An ear tattoo (enhanced for clarity).

have a secure "O" ring attachment; you also can explore the type of tag that slides right onto the collar.

In addition to the ID tag, which every dog should wear even if identified by another method, two other forms of identification have become popular: microchipping and tattooing. In microchipping, a tiny scannable chip is painlessly inserted under the dog's skin. The number is registered to you so that, if your lost dog turns up at a veterinary clinic or a shelter, the chip can be scanned to retrieve your contact information.

The advantage of the microchip is that it is a permanent form of ID, but there are some factors to consider. Several different companies make microchips, and not all are compatible with

your dog on lead when out and about in public places. If your dog is not properly identified, however, you are overlooking a major aspect of his safety. We hope to never be in a situation where our dog is missing, but we should practice prevention in the unfortunate case that this happens; identification greatly increases the chances of your dog's being returned to you.

There are several ways to identify your dog. First, the traditional dog tag should be a staple in your dog's wardrobe, attached to his everyday collar. Tags can be made of sturdy plastic and various metals and should include your contact information so that a person who finds the dog can get in touch with you right away to arrange his return. Many people today enjoy the wide range of decorative tags available, so have fun and create a tag to match your dog's personality. Of course, it is important that the tag stays on the collar, so

PET OR STRAY?

Besides the obvious benefit of providing your contact information to whoever finds your lost dog, an ID tag makes your dog more approachable and more likely to be recovered. A strange dog wandering the neighborhood without a collar and tags will look like a stray, while the collar and tags indicate that the dog is someone's pet. Even if the ID tags become detached from the collar, the collar alone will make a person more likely to pick up the dog.

the others' scanning devices. It's best to find a company with a universal microchip that can be read by scanners made by other companies as well. It won't do any good to have the dog chipped if the information cannot be retrieved. Also, not every humane society, shelter and clinic is equipped with a scanner, although more and more facilities are equipping themselves. In fact, many shelters microchip dogs that they adopt out to new homes.

Because the microchip is not visible to the eye, the dog must wear a tag that states that he is microchipped so that whoever picks him up will know to have him scanned or to call the microchip registry. He of course also should have a tag with your contact information in case his chip cannot be read. Humane societies and veterinary clinics offer microchipping service, which is usually very affordable.

Though less popular than microchipping, tattooing is another permanent method of ID for dogs. Most vets perform this service, and there are also clinics that perform dog tattooing. This is also an affordable procedure and one that will not cause much discomfort for the dog. It is best to put the tattoo in a visible area, such as the ear or the groin area, to deter theft. It is sad to say that there are cases of dogs being stolen and sold to research labora-

tories, but such laboratories will not accept tattooed dogs.

To ensure that the tattoo is effective in aiding your dog's return to you, the tattoo number must be registered with a national organization. That way, when someone finds a tattooed dog, a phone call to the registry will quickly match the dog with his owner.

HIT THE ROAD
If you are lucky the breeder has already taken the puppies in his

FEEDING IN HOT WEATHER
Even the most dedicated chow hound may have less of an appetite when the weather is hot or humid. If your dog leaves more of his food behind than usual, adjust his portions until the weather and his appetite return to normal. Never leave the uneaten portion in the bowl, hoping he will return to finish it, because higher temperatures encourage food spoilage and bacterial growth.

The back of this car has been partitioned off to give the dogs a safe area in which to ride and to keep them from disturbing the driver.

staying at home when you are on the road.

Car travel with your Welsh Springer Spaniel may be limited to necessity only, such as trips to the vet, or you may bring your dog along almost everywhere you go. This will depend much on your individual dog and how he reacts to rides in the car. You can begin desensitizing your dog to car travel as a pup so that it's something that he's used to. Still, some dogs suffer from motion sickness. Your vet may prescribe a medication for this if trips in the car pose a problem for your dog. At the very least, you will need to get him to the vet, so he will need to tolerate these trips with the least amount of hassle possible.

Of course, safety is a concern for dogs in the car. First, he must travel securely, not left loose to roam about the car where he could be injured or distract the driver. A young pup can be held by a passenger initially but should soon graduate to a travel crate, which can be the same crate he uses in the home if it fits in your car. Other options include a car harness (like a seat belt for dogs) and partitioning the back of the car with a gate made for this purpose.

Bring along what you will need for the dog. He should wear his collar and ID tags, of course, and you should bring his leash,

car for a visit to the vet or just for a ride, so that when you come to take your puppy home he knows what it is like to be in a car. You will find that most spaniels love to ride in the car.

The best way to accustom your puppy to traveling in the car is by doing it gradually. Start by putting the puppy in the car in his crate while you sit behind the steering wheel. Talk to him and tell him how much he will enjoy this. Repeat this the next day and start the car; let the engine run for a couple of minutes. The next day you should drive around the block and, day by day, slowly extend your trips. Start to take him on your errands or just for drives around town. By this time it will be easy to tell whether your dog is a born traveler or would prefer

water (and food if a long trip) and clean-up materials for potty breaks and in case of motion sickness. Always keep your dog on his leash when you make stops, and never leave him alone in the car. Many a dog has died from the heat inside a closed car; this does not take much time at all. Leaving windows cracked open is unsafe too, as the dog could try to escape or could become a target for thieves.

BOARDING

Today there are many options for dog owners who need someone to care for their dogs in certain circumstances. While many think of boarding their dogs as something to do when away on vacation, many others use the services of doggie "daycare" facilities, dropping their dogs off to spend the day while they are at work. Many of these facilities offer both long-term and daily care. Many go beyond just boarding and cater to all sorts of needs, with on-site grooming, veterinary care, training classes and even "web-cams" where owners can log onto the Internet and check out what their dogs are up to. Most dogs enjoy the activity and time spent with other dogs.

Before you need to use such a service, check out the ones in your area. Make visits to see the facilities, meet the staff, discuss fees and available services and see

whether this is a place where you think your dog will be happy. It is best to do your research in advance so that you're not stuck at the last minute, forced into making a rushed decision without knowing whether the kennel that you've chosen meets your standards. You also can check with your vet's office to see whether they offer boarding for their clients or can recommend a good kennel in the area.

The kennel will need to see proof of your dog's health records and vaccinations so as not to spread illness from dog to dog. Your dog also will need proper identification. Owners usually experience some separation anxiety the first time they have to leave their dog in someone else's care, so it's reassuring to know that the kennel you choose is run by experienced, caring, true dog people.

Imagine if these dogs were not trained to walk on lead without pulling?

BASIC TRAINING PRINCIPLES: PUPPY VS. ADULT

There's a big difference between training an adult dog and training a young puppy. With a young puppy, everything is new! At eight to ten weeks of age, he will be experiencing many things, and he has nothing with which to compare these experiences. Up to this point, he has been with his dam and littermates, not one-on-one with people except in his interactions with his breeder and visitors to the litter.

SMILE WHEN YOU ORDER ME AROUND!

While trainers recommend practicing with your dog every day, it's perfectly acceptable to take a "mental health day" off. It's better not to train the dog on days when you're in a sour mood. Your bad attitude or lack of interest will be sensed by your dog, and he will respond accordingly. Studies show that dogs are well tuned in to their humans' emotions. Be conscious of how you use your voice when talking to your dog. Raising your voice or shouting will only erode your dog's trust in you as his trainer and master.

When you first bring the puppy home, he is eager to please you. This means that he accepts doing things your way. During the next couple of months, he will absorb the basis of everything he needs to know for the rest of his life. This early age is even referred to as the "sponge" stage. After that, for the next 18 months, it's up to you to reinforce good manners by building on the foundation that you've established. Once your puppy is reliable in basic commands and behavior and has reached the appropriate age, you may gradually introduce him to some of the interesting sports, games and activities available to pet owners and their dogs.

Raising your puppy is a family affair. Each member of the family must know what rules to set forth for the puppy and how to use the same one-word commands to mean exactly the same thing every time. Even if yours is a large family, one person will soon be considered by the pup to be the leader, the alpha person in his pack, the "boss" who must be obeyed. Often that highly regarded person turns out to be the one who feeds the puppy.

Food ranks very high on the puppy's list of important things! That's why your puppy is rewarded with small treats along with verbal praise when he responds to you correctly. As the puppy learns to do what you want him to do, the food rewards are gradually eliminated and only the praise remains. If you were to keep up with the food treats, you could have two problems on your hands—an obese dog and a beggar.

Training begins the minute your Welsh Springer Spaniel puppy steps through the doorway of your home, so don't make the mistake of putting the puppy on the floor and telling him by your actions to "Go for it! Run wild!" Even if this is your first puppy, you must act as if you know what you're doing: be the boss. An uncertain pup may be terrified to move, while a bold one will be ready to take you at your word and start plotting to destroy the house! Before you picked up your puppy, you decided where his own special place would be, and that's where to put him when you first arrive home. Give him a house tour after he has investigated his area and had a nap and a bathroom "pit stop."

It's worth mentioning here that, if you've adopted an adult dog that is completely trained to your liking, lucky you! You're off the hook! However, if that dog

spent his life up to this point in a kennel, or even in a good home but without any real training, be prepared to tackle the job ahead. A dog three years of age or older with no previous training cannot be blamed for not knowing what he was never taught. While the dog is trying to understand and learn your rules, at the same time he has to unlearn many of his previously self-taught habits and general view of the world.

Working with a professional trainer will speed up your progress with an adopted adult

A well-trained Welsh Springer Spaniel is an enjoyable companion and will be welcome wherever dogs are allowed. Ch. Fairwinds Son of a Sailor and owner Beth Holmes enjoy lunch at a Beverly Hills café.

Best buddies! The gregarious and affectionate Welshie is a family companion beyond compare.

dog. You'll need patience, too. Some new rules may be close to impossible for the dog to accept. After all, he's been successful so far by doing everything his way! (Patience again.) He may agree with your instruction for a few days and then slip back into his old ways, so you must be just as consistent and understanding in your teaching as you would be with a puppy. (More patience needed yet again!) Your dog has to learn to pay attention to your voice, your family, the daily routine, new smells, new sounds and, in some cases, even a new climate.

One of the most important things to find out about a newly adopted adult dog is his reaction to children (yours and others), strangers and your friends and how he acts upon meeting other dogs. If he was not socialized with

dogs as a puppy, this could be a major problem. This does not mean that he's a "bad" dog, a vicious dog or an aggressive dog; rather, it means that he has no idea how to read another dog's body language. There's no way for him to tell whether the other dog is a friend or foe. Survival instinct takes over, telling him to attack first and ask questions later. This definitely calls for professional help and, even then, may not be a behavior that can be corrected 100% reliably (or even at all). If you have a puppy, this is why it is so very important to introduce your young puppy properly to other puppies and "dog-friendly" adult dogs.

HOUSE-TRAINING YOUR WELSH SPRINGER SPANIEL
Dogs are tactility-oriented when it comes to house-training. In other words, they respond to the surface on which they are given approval to eliminate. The choice is yours (the dog's version is in parentheses): The lawn (including the neighbors' lawns)? A bare patch of

TIDY BOY

Clean by nature, dogs do not like to soil their dens, which in effect are their crates or sleeping quarters. Unless not feeling well, dogs will not defecate or urinate in their crates. Crate training capitalizes on the dog's natural desire to keep his den clean. Be conscientious about giving the puppy as many opportunities to relieve himself outdoors as possible. Reward the puppy for correct behavior. Praise him and pat him whenever he "goes" in the correct location. Even the tidiest of puppies can have potty accidents, so be patient and dedicate more energy to helping your puppy achieve a clean lifestyle.

earth under a tree (where people like to sit and relax in the summertime)? Concrete steps or patio (all sidewalks, garages and basement floors)? The curbside (watch out for cars)? A small area of crushed stone in a corner of the yard (mine!)? The latter is the best choice if you can manage it, because it will remain strictly for the dog's use and is easy to keep clean.

You can start out with paper-training indoors and switch over to an outdoor surface as the puppy matures and gains control over his need to eliminate. For the naysayers, don't worry—this won't mean that the dog will soil on every piece of newspaper lying around the house. You are training him to go outside, remember? Starting out by paper-training often is the only choice for a city dog.

WHEN YOUR PUPPY'S "GOT TO GO"
Your puppy's need to relieve himself is seemingly non-stop, but signs of improvement will be seen each week. From 8 to 10 weeks old, the puppy will have to be taken outside every time he wakes up, about 10 to 15 minutes after every meal and after every period of play—all day long, from first thing in the morning until his bedtime. That's a total of ten or more trips per day to teach the puppy where it's okay to relieve himself. With that schedule in mind, you can see that house-training a young puppy is not a part-time job. It requires someone to be home all day.

Eventually your Welshie will have a favorite spot in which he will relieve himself.

If that seems overwhelming or impossible, do a little planning. For example, plan to pick up your puppy at the start of a vacation period. If you can't get home in the middle of the day, plan to hire a dog-sitter or ask a neighbor to come over to take the pup outside, feed him his lunch and then take him out again about ten or so minutes after he's eaten. Also make arrangements with that or another person to be your "emergency" contact if you have to stay late on the job. Remind yourself—repeatedly—that this hectic schedule improves as the puppy gets older.

HOME WITHIN A HOME

Your Welsh Springer Spaniel puppy needs to be confined to one secure, puppy-proof area when no one is able to watch his every move. Generally the kitchen is the place of choice because the floor is washable. Likewise, it's a busy family area that will accustom the pup to a variety of noises, everything from pots and pans to the telephone, blender and dishwasher. He will also be enchanted by the smell of your cooking (and will never be critical when you burn something). An exercise pen (also called an "expen," a puppy version of a playpen) within the room of choice is also helpful for confining a young pup. He can see out and has a certain amount of space in which to run about, but he is safe from dangerous things like electrical cords, heating units, trash containers or open kitchen-supply cabinets. Also keep all medications out of reach. Place the pen where the puppy will not get a blast of heat or air conditioning.

In the pen, you can put a few toys, his bed (which can be his crate if the dimensions of pen and crate are compatible) and a few layers of newspaper in one small corner, just in case. A water bowl can be hung at a convenient height on the side of the ex-pen so it won't become a splashing pool for an innovative puppy. His food dish can go on the floor, next to but not under the water bowl.

Crates are something that pet owners are at last getting used to for their dogs. Wild or domestic

Crate training has benefits for both dog and owner, but this isn't exactly what we mean!

canines have always preferred to sleep in den-like safe spots, and that is exactly what the crate provides. How often have you seen adult dogs that choose to sleep under a table or chair even though they have full run of the house? It's the den connection.

In your "happy" voice, use the word "Crate" every time you put the pup into his den. If he's new to a crate, toss in a small biscuit

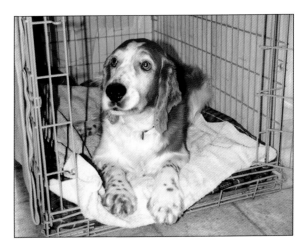

for him to chase the first few times. At night, after he's been outside, he should sleep in his crate. The crate may be kept in his designated area at night or, if you want to be sure to hear those wake-up yips in the morning, put the crate in a corner of your bedroom. However, don't make any response whatsoever to whining or crying. If he's completely ignored, he'll settle down and get to sleep.

Good bedding for a young puppy is an old folded bath towel or an old blanket, something that is easily washable and disposable if necessary ("accidents" will happen!). Never put newspaper in the puppy's crate. Also those old ideas about adding a clock to replace his mother's heartbeat or a hot-water bottle to replace her warmth, are just that—old ideas. The clock could drive the puppy nuts, and the hot-water bottle

This Welshie seems to be right at home in his cozy crate. Once the dog is reliably trained, the crate door can be left open so the dog can come and go as he pleases.

Never use newspapers to line the crate. Litters of pups are often raised on newspapers and therefore associate the papers with relieving themselves.

could end up as a very soggy waterbed! An extremely good breeder would have introduced your puppy to the crate by letting two pups sleep together for a couple of nights, followed by several nights alone. How thankful you will be if you found that breeder!

Safe toys in the pup's crate or area will keep him occupied, but monitor their condition closely. Discard any toys that show signs of being chewed to bits. Squeaky parts, bits of stuffing or plastic or any other small pieces can cause intestinal blockage or possibly choking if swallowed.

PROGRESSING WITH POTTY-TRAINING
After you've taken your puppy out and he has relieved himself in the area you've selected, he can have some free time with the family as long as there is some-one responsible for watching him. That doesn't mean just someone in the same room who is watching TV or busy on the computer, but one person who is doing nothing other than keeping an eye on the pup, playing with him on the floor and helping him understand his position in the pack.

LEASH TRAINING
House-training and leash training go hand in hand, literally. When taking your puppy outside to do his business, lead him there on his leash. Unless an emergency potty run is called for, do not whisk the puppy up into your arms and take him outside. If you have a fenced yard, you have the advantage of letting the puppy loose to go out, but it's better to put the dog on the leash and take him to his designated place in the yard until he is reliably house-trained. Taking the puppy for a walk is the best way to house-train a dog. The dog will associate the walk with his time to relieve himself, and the exercise of walking stimulates the dog's bowels and bladder. Dogs that are not trained to relieve themselves on a walk may hold it until they get back home, which of course defeats half the purpose of the walk.

CANINE DEVELOPMENT SCHEDULE

It is important to understand how and at what age a puppy develops into adulthood. If you are a puppy owner, consult this Canine Development Schedule to determine the stage of development your puppy is currently experiencing. This knowledge will help you as you work with the puppy in the weeks and months ahead.

PERIOD	AGE	CHARACTERISTICS
FIRST TO THIRD	BIRTH TO SEVEN WEEKS	Puppy needs food, sleep and warmth and responds to simple and gentle touching. Needs mother for security and disciplining. Needs littermates for learning and interacting with other dogs. Pup learns to function within a pack and learns pack order of dominance. Begin socializing pup with adults and children for short periods. Pup begins to become aware of his environment.
FOURTH	EIGHT TO TWELVE WEEKS	Brain is fully developed. Pup needs socializing with outside world. Remove from mother and littermates. Needs to change from canine pack to human pack. Human dominance necessary. Fear period occurs between 8 and 10 weeks. Avoid fright and pain.
FIFTH	THIRTEEN TO SIXTEEN WEEKS	Training and formal obedience should begin. Less association with other dogs, more with people, places, situations. Period will pass easily if you remember this is pup's change-to-adolescence time. Be firm and fair. Flight instinct prominent. Permissiveness and over-disciplining can do permanent damage. Praise for good behavior.
JUVENILE	FOUR TO EIGHT MONTHS	Another fear period about 7 to 8 months of age. It passes quickly, but be cautious of fright and pain. Sexual maturity reached. Dominant traits established. Dog should understand sit, down, come and stay by now.

NOTE: THESE ARE APPROXIMATE TIME FRAMES. ALLOW FOR INDIVIDUAL DIFFERENCES IN PUPPIES.

When this pup wakes up from naptime, it immediately will be potty time. Supervision is crucial to both the pup's safety and house-training success.

This first taste of freedom will let you begin to set the house rules. If you don't want the dog on the furniture, now is the time to prevent his first attempts to jump up onto the couch. The word to use in this case is "Off," not "Down." "Down" is the word you will use to teach the down position, which is something entirely different.

Most corrections at this stage come in the form of simply distracting the puppy. Instead of telling him "No" for "Don't chew the carpet," distract the chomping puppy with a toy and he'll forget about the carpet.

As you are playing with the pup, do not forget to watch him closely and pay attention to his body language. Whenever you see him begin to circle or sniff, take the puppy outside to relieve himself. If you are paper-training, put him back into his confined area on the newspapers. In either case, praise him as he eliminates while he actually is in the act of relieving himself. Three seconds after he has finished is too late! You'll be praising him for running toward you, picking up a toy or whatever he may be doing at that moment, and that's not what you want to be praising him for. Timing is a vital tool in all dog training. Use it.

Remove soiled newspapers immediately and replace them with clean ones. You may want to take a small piece of soiled paper and place it in the middle of the new clean papers, as the scent will attract him to that spot when it's time to go again. That

> **EXTRA! EXTRA!**
> The headlines read: "Puppy Piddles Here!" Breeders commonly use newspapers to line their whelping pens, so puppies learn to associate newspapers with relieving themselves. Do not use newspapers to line your pup's crate, as this will signal to your puppy that it is OK to urinate in his crate. If you choose to paper-train your puppy, you will layer newspapers on a section of the floor near the door he uses to go outside. You should encourage the puppy to use the papers to relieve himself, and bring him there whenever you see him getting ready to go. Little by little, you will reduce the size of the newspaper-covered area so that the puppy will learn to relieve himself "on the other side of the door."

DAILY SCHEDULE
How many relief trips does your puppy need per day? A puppy up to the age of 14 weeks will need to go outside about 8 to 12 times per day! You will have to take the pup out any time he starts sniffing around the floor or turning in small circles, as well as after naps, meals, games and lessons or whenever he's released from his crate. Once the puppy is 14 to 22 weeks of age, he will require only 6 to 8 relief trips. At the ages of 22 to 32 weeks, the puppy will require about 5 to 7 trips. Adult dogs typically require 4 relief trips per day, in the morning, afternoon, evening and late at night.

for you, that is. Just stand there until he urinates and defecates. Move him a few feet in one direction or another if he's just sitting there looking at you, but remember that this is neither playtime nor time for a walk. This is strictly a business trip! Then, as he circles and squats (remember your timing!), give him a quiet "Good dog" as praise. If you start to jump for joy, ecstatic over his performance, he'll do one of two things: either he will stop midstream, as it were, or he'll do it again for you—in the house—and expect you to be just as delighted!

scent attraction is why it's so important to clean up any messes made in the house by using a product specially made to eliminate the odor of dog urine and droppings. Regular household cleansers won't do the trick. Pet shops sell the best pet deodorizers. Invest in the largest container you can find.

Scent attraction eventually will lead your pup to his chosen spot outdoors; this is the basis of outdoor training. When you take your puppy outside to relieve himself, use a one-word command such as "Outside" or "Go-potty" (that's one word to the puppy!) as you attach his leash. Then lead him to his spot. Now comes the hard part—hard

This Welshie puppy knows the routine— he's gone out to do his business and now it's time to come back in!

KEEPING THE PACK ORDERLY
Discipline is a form of training that brings order to life. For example, military discipline is what allows the soldiers in an army to work as one. Discipline is a form of teaching and, in dogs, is the basis of how the successful pack operates. Each member knows his place in the pack and all respect the leader, or alpha dog. It is essential for your puppy that you establish this type of relationship, with you as the alpha, or leader. It is a form of social coexistence that all canines recognize and accept. Discipline, therefore, is never to be confused with punishment. When you teach your puppy how you want him to behave, and he behaves properly

Don't leave your Welshie waiting on the wrong side of the door. Your dog will clue you in when he needs to go out; don't ignore his signs!

Give him five minutes or so and, if he doesn't go in that time, take him back indoors to his confined area and try again in another ten minutes, or immediately if you see him sniffing and circling. By careful observation, you'll soon work out a successful schedule.

Accidents, by the way, are just that—accidents. Clean them up quickly and thoroughly, without comment, after the puppy has been taken outside to finish his business and then put back into his area or crate. If you witness an accident in progress, say "No!" in a stern voice and get the pup outdoors immediately. No punishment is needed. You and your puppy are just learning each other's language, and sometimes it's easy to miss a puppy's message. Chalk it up to experience and watch more closely from now on.

POTTY COMMAND
Most dogs love to please their masters; there are no bounds to what dogs will do to make their owners happy. The potty command is a good example of this theory. If eliminating on command makes the master happy, then more power to him. Puppies will obligingly piddle if it really makes their keepers smile. Some owners can be creative about which word they will use to command their dogs to relieve themselves. Some popular choices are "Potty," "Tinkle," "Piddle," "Let's go," "Hurry up" and "Toilet." Give the command every time your puppy goes into position and the puppy will begin to associate his business with the command.

and you praise him for it, you are disciplining him with a form of positive reinforcement.

For a dog, rewards come in the form of praise, a smile, a cheerful tone of voice, a few friendly pats or a rub of the ears. Rewards are also small food treats. Obviously, that does not mean bits of regular dog food. Instead, treats are very small bits of special things like cheese or pieces of soft dog treats. The idea is to reward the dog with something very small that he can taste and swallow, providing instant positive reinforcement. If he has to take time to chew the treat, he will have forgotten what he did to earn it by the time he is finished!

Your puppy should never be physically punished. The displeasure shown on your face and in your voice is sufficient to signal to the pup that he has done something wrong. He wants to please everyone higher up on the social ladder, especially his leader, so a scowl and harsh voice will take care of the error. Growling out the word "Shame!" when the pup is caught in the act of doing something wrong is better than the repetitive "No." Some dogs hear "No" so often that they begin to think it's their name! By the way, do not use the dog's name when you're correcting him. His name is reserved to get his attention for something pleasant about to take place.

There are punishments that have nothing to do with you. For example, your dog may think that chasing cats is one reason for his existence. You can try to stop it as much as you like but without success, because it's such fun for the dog. But one good hissing, spitting swipe of a cat's claws across the dog's nose will put an end to the game forever. Intervene only when your dog's eyeball is seriously at risk. Cat scratches can cause permanent damage to an innocent but annoying puppy.

PUPPY KINDERGARTEN

COLLAR AND LEASH

Before you begin your Welsh Springer Spaniel puppy's education, he must be used to his collar and leash. Choose a collar for your puppy that is secure, but not heavy or bulky. He won't enjoy

SHOULD WE ENROLL?
If you have the means and the time, you should definitely take your dog to obedience classes. Begin with puppy kindergarten classes in which puppies of all sizes learn basic lessons while getting the opportunity to meet and greet each other; it's as much about socialization as it is about good manners. What you learn in class you can practice at home. And if you goof up in practice, you'll get help in the next session.

A puppy must be taught which behaviors are unacceptable. A Welshie (or any!) puppy sees no harm in a playful nip; it's up to you to teach him right from wrong.

shorter because you don't want him to roam away from his area. The shorter leash will also be the one to use when you walk the puppy.

If you've been wise enough to enroll in a puppy kindergarten training class, suggestions will be made as to the best collar and leash for your young puppy. I say "wise" because your puppy will be in a class with puppies in his age range (up to five months old) of all breeds and sizes. It's the perfect way for him to learn the right way (and the wrong way) to interact with other dogs as well as their people. You cannot teach your puppy how to interpret another dog's sign language. For a first-time puppy owner, these socialization classes are invaluable. For experienced dog owners,

training if he's uncomfortable. A flat buckle collar is fine for everyday wear and for initial puppy training. For older dogs, there are several types of training collars such as the martingale, which is a double loop that tightens slightly around the neck, or the head collar, which is similar to a horse's halter. Chain choke collars are not often used with Welsh Springers. A simple buckle collar is fine for most dogs.

A lightweight 6-foot woven cotton or nylon training leash is preferred by most trainers because it is easy to fold up in your hand and comfortable to hold because there is a certain amount of give to it. There are lessons where the dog will start off 6 feet away from you at the end of the leash. The leash used to take the puppy outside to relieve himself is

BASIC PRINCIPLES OF DOG TRAINING

1. Start training early. A young puppy is ready, willing and able.
2. Timing is your all-important tool. Praise at the exact time that the dog responds correctly. Pay close attention.
3. Patience is almost as important as timing!
4. Repeat! The same word has to mean the same thing every time.
5. In the beginning, praise all correct behavior verbally, along with treats and petting.

to catch him whenever he is about to sit and, as his backside nears the floor, say "Sit, good dog!" That's positive reinforcement and, if your timing is sharp, he will learn that what he's doing at that second is connected to your saying "Sit" and that you think he's clever for doing it!

Another method is to start with the puppy on his leash in front of you. Show him a treat in the palm of your right hand.

they are a real boon to further training.

On leash and sitting at attention, this Welshie is ready to learn something new.

ATTENTION

You've been using the dog's name since the minute you picked him up from the breeder, so you should be able to get his attention by saying his name—with a big smile and in an excited tone of voice. His response will be the puppy equivalent of "Here I am! What are we going to do?" Your immediate response (if you haven't guessed by now) is "Good dog." Rewarding him at the moment he pays attention to you teaches him the proper way to respond when he hears his name.

EXERCISES FOR A BASIC CANINE EDUCATION

THE SIT EXERCISE

There are several ways to teach the puppy to sit. The first one is

A pair of handsome young Welsh Springers with their collars and leads.

"Sit" and have him sit. You thereby will have taught him two things at the same time. Both the verbal command and the motion of the hand are signals for the sit. Your puppy is watching you almost more than he is listening to you, so what you do is just as important as what you say.

Don't save any of these drills only for training sessions. Use them as much as possible at odd times during a normal day. The dog should always sit before being given his food dish. He should sit to let you go through a doorway first, when the doorbell rings or

Bring your hand up under his nose and, almost in slow motion, move your hand up and back so his nose goes up in the air and his head tilts back as he follows the treat in your hand. At that point, he will have to either sit or fall over, so as his back legs buckle under, say "Sit, good dog," and then give him the treat and lots of praise. You may have to begin with your hand lightly running up his chest, actually lifting his chin up until he sits. Some (usually older) dogs require gentle pressure on their hindquarters with the left hand, in which case the dog should be on your left side. Puppies gener-ally do not appreciate this physi-cal dominance.

After a few times, you should be able to show the dog a treat in the open palm of your hand, raise your hand waist-high as you say

TIPS FOR TRAINING AND SAFETY

1. Whether on- or off-leash, practice only in a fenced area.
2. Remove the training collar when the training session is over.
3. Don't try to break up a dogfight.
4. "Come," "Leave it" and "Wait" are safety commands.
5. The dog belongs in a crate or behind a barrier when riding in the car.
6. Don't ignore the dog's first sign of aggression. Aggression only gets worse, so take it seriously.
7. Keep the faces of children and dogs separated.
8. Pay attention to what the dog is chewing.
9. Keep the vet's number near your phone.
10. "Okay" is a useful release command.

READY, SIT, GO!
On your marks, get set: train! Most professional trainers agree that the sit command is the place to start your dog's formal education. Sitting is a natural posture for most dogs, and they respond to the sit exercise willingly and readily. For every lesson, begin with the sit command so that you start out with a successful exercise; likewise, you should practice the sit command at the end of every lesson as well because you always want to end on a high note.

when you stop to speak to someone on the street.

THE DOWN EXERCISE
Before beginning to teach the down command, you must consider how the dog feels about this exercise. To him, being "down" is a submissive position. Being flat on the floor with you standing over him is not his idea of fun. It's up to you to let him know that, while it may not be fun, the reward of your approval is worth his effort.

Start with the puppy on your left side in a sit position. Hold the leash right above his collar in your left hand. Have an extra-special treat, such as a small piece of cooked chicken or hot dog, in your right hand. Place it at the end of the pup's nose and steadily move your hand down and

forward along the ground. Hold the leash to prevent a sudden lunge for the food. As the puppy goes into the down position, say "Down" very gently.

The difficulty with this exercise is twofold: it's both the submissive aspect and the fact that most people say the word "Down" as if they were drill sergeants in charge of recruits! So issue the command sweetly, give him the treat and have the pup maintain the down position for several seconds. If he tries to get up immediately, place your hands on his shoulders and press down gently, giving him a very quiet "Good dog." As you progress with this lesson, increase the "down time" until he will hold it until you say "Okay" (his cue for release). Practice this one in the house at various times throughout the day.

By increasing the length of time during which the dog must maintain the down position, you'll find many uses for it. For example, he can lie at your feet in the vet's office or anywhere that both of you have to wait, when you are on the phone, while the family is eating and so forth. If you progress to training for competitive obedience, he'll already be all set for the exercise called the "long down."

THE STAY EXERCISE
You can teach your Welsh Springer Spaniel to stay in the sit,

can hold it for at least 30 seconds without moving. After about a week of success, move out on your right foot and take two steps before turning to face the dog. Give the "Stay" hand signal (left palm back toward the dog's head) as you leave. He gets the treat when you return and he holds the sit/stay. Increase the distance that you walk away from him before turning until you reach the length of your training leash. But don't rush it! Go back to the beginning if he moves before he should. No matter what the lesson, never be upset by having to back up for a few days. The repetition and practice are what will make your dog reliable in these commands. It won't do any good to move on to something more difficult if the command is not mastered at the easier levels.

Your dog must be paying attention to you before he can learn anything. During lessons, make sure that his focus is on you and the lesson.

down and stand positions. To teach the sit/stay, have the dog sit on your left side. Hold the leash at waist level in your left hand and let the dog know that you have a treat in your closed right hand. Step forward on your right foot as you say "Stay." Immediately turn and stand directly in front of the dog, keeping your right hand up high so he'll keep his eye on the treat hand and maintain the sit position for a count of five. Return to your original position and offer the reward.

Increase the length of the sit/stay each time until the dog

DOWN

"Down" is a harsh-sounding word and a submissive posture in dog body language, thus presenting two obstacles in teaching the down command. When the dog is about to flop down on his own, tell him "Good down." Pups that are not good about being handled learn better by having food lowered in front of them. A dog that trusts you can be gently guided into position. When you give the command "Down," be sure to say it sweetly!

Above all, even if you do get frustrated, never let your puppy know! Always keep a positive, upbeat attitude during training, which will transmit to your dog for positive results.

The down/stay is taught in the same way once the dog is completely reliable and steady with the down command. Again, don't rush it. With the dog in the down position on your left side, step out on your right foot as you say "Stay." Return by walking around the back of the dog and into your original position. While you are training, it's okay to murmur something like "Hold on" to encourage him to stay put. When the dog will stay without moving when you are at a distance of 3 or 4 feet, begin to increase the length of time before

you return. Be sure he holds the down on your return until you say "Okay." At that point, he gets his treat—just so he'll remember for next time that it's not over until it's over.

THE COME EXERCISE

No command is more important to the safety of your Welsh Springer Spaniel than "Come." It is what you should say every single time you see the puppy running toward you: "Dylan, come! Good dog." During playtime, run a few feet away from the puppy and turn and tell him to "Come" as he is already running to you. You can go so far as to teach your puppy two things at once if you squat down and hold out your arms. As the pup gets close to you and you're saying "Good dog," bring your right arm in about waist high. Now he's also learning the hand signal, an excel-

A dog can also learn to stay in a standing position; this is a requirement for show dogs, as they must stand in the ring for evaluation by the judge.

I WILL FOLLOW YOU

Obedience isn't just a classroom activity. In your home you have many great opportunities to teach your dog polite manners. Allowing your pet on the bed or furniture elevates him to your level, which is not a good idea when trying to establish yourself as leader (the word is "Off!"). Use the "umbilical cord" method, keeping your dog on lead so he has to go with you wherever you go. You sit, he sits. You walk, he heels. You stop, he sit/stays. Everywhere you go, he's with you, but you go first!

A properly trained Welsh Springer Spaniel should react energetically when he hears the command "Come."

Never call the dog to come to you—with or without his name—if you are angry or intend to correct him for some misbehavior. When correcting the pup, you go to him. Your dog must always connect "Come" with something pleasant and with your approval; then you can rely on his response.

Puppies, like children, have notoriously short attention spans, so don't overdo it with any of the training. Keep each lesson short. Break it up with a quick run around the yard or a ball toss, repeat the lesson and quit as soon as the pup gets it right. That way, you will always end with a "Good dog."

lent device should you be on the phone when you need to get him to come to you! You'll also both be one step ahead when you enter obedience classes.

When the puppy responds to your well-timed "Come," try it with the puppy on the training leash. This time, catch him off-guard, while he's sniffing a leaf or watching a bird: "Dylan, come!" You may have to pause for a split second after his name to be sure you have his attention. If the puppy shows any sign of confusion, give the leash a mild jerk and take a couple of steps backward. Do not repeat the command. In this case, you should say "Good come" as he reaches you.

That's an important rule of training. Each command word is given just once. Anything more is nagging. You'll also notice that all commands are one word only. Even when they are actually two words, you say them as one.

Life isn't perfect and neither are puppies. A time will come, often around ten months of age, when he'll become "selectively deaf" or choose to "forget" his name. He may respond by wagging his tail (and even seeming to smile at you) with a look that says "Make me!" Laugh, throw his favorite toy and skip the lesson you had planned. Pups will be pups!

THE HEEL EXERCISE

The second most important command to teach, after the come, is the heel. When you are walking your growing puppy, you need to be in control. Besides, it looks terrible to be pulled and yanked down the street, and it's not much fun either. Your eight- to ten-week-old puppy will probably follow you everywhere, but that's his natural instinct, not your control over the situation. However, any time he does follow you, you can say "Heel" and be ahead of the game, as he will learn to associate this command with the action of following you before you even begin teaching him to heel.

There is a very precise, almost military, procedure for teaching your dog to heel. As with all other obedience training, begin with the dog on your left side. He will be in a very nice sit and you will have the training leash across your chest, about waist-high. Hold the loop and folded leash in your right hand. Pick up the slack leash above the dog in your left hand and hold it loosely at your side. Step out on your left foot as you say "Heel." If the puppy does not move, give a gentle tug or pat your left leg to get him started. If he surges ahead of you, stop and pull him back gently until he is at your side. Tell him to sit and begin again.

Walk a few steps and stop while the puppy is correctly beside you. Tell him to sit and give mild verbal praise. (More enthusiastic praise will encourage him to think the lesson is over.) Repeat the lesson, increasing the number of steps you take only as long as the dog is heeling nicely beside you. When you end the lesson, have him hold the sit, then give him the

"Okay" to let him know that this is the end of the lesson. Praise him so that he knows he did a good job.

The cure for excessive pulling (a common problem) is to stop when the dog is no more than 2 or 3 feet ahead of you. Guide him back into position and begin again. With a really determined puller, try switching to a head collar. When used properly, this will automatically turn the pup's head toward you so you can bring him back easily to the heel position. Another alternative is to try a no-pull harness, which is available in several styles and will protect the larynx and trachea from injury. Give quiet, reassuring praise every time the leash goes slack and he's staying with you.

Staying and heeling can take a lot out of a dog, so provide play-time and free-running exercise to shake off the stress when the lessons are over. You don't want

COME AND GET IT!
The come command is your dog's safety signal. Until he is 99% perfect in responding, don't use the come command if you cannot enforce it. Practice on leash with treats or squeakers, or whenever the dog is running to you. Never call him to come to you if he is to be corrected for misbehaving. Reward the dog with a treat and happy praise whenever he comes to you.

Showing off the breed's powerful gait, this Welshie is heeling to perfection in the show ring.

something brand-new that you want to teach him. Keep up the praise and you'll always have a "good dog."

OBEDIENCE CLASSES

The advantages of an obedience class are that your dog will have to learn amid the distractions of other people and dogs and that your mistakes will be quickly corrected by the trainer. Teaching your dog along with a qualified instructor and other handlers who may have more dog experience than you is another plus of the class environment. The instructor and other handlers can help you to find the most efficient way of teaching your dog a command or exercise. It's often easier to learn from other people's mistakes than your own. You will also learn all of the requirements for competitive obedience trials, in which you can earn titles and go on to advanced jumping and retrieving exercises, which are fun for many dogs. Obedience classes build the foundation needed for many other canine activities (in which we humans are allowed to participate, too!).

him to associate training with all work and no fun.

TAPERING OFF TIDBITS

Your dog has been watching you—and the hand that treats—throughout all of his lessons, and now it's time to break the treat habit. Begin by giving him treats at the end of each lesson only. Then start to give a treat after the end of only some of the lessons. At the end of every lesson, as well as during the lessons, be consistent with the praise. Your pup now doesn't know whether he'll get a treat or not, but he should keep performing well just in case! Finally, you will stop giving treat rewards entirely. Save them for

GUNDOG TRAINING

The spaniel's duties in the field consist of working close to the sportsman, to quest for game and to flush it and retrieve it when called upon to do so. The springer is the dog for the rough shooter, i.e., the man who goes out by himself in search of game, be it fur or feather. The Welsh Springer Spaniel has often been referred to as "the working man's spaniel." He is not bred for glamour but purely and exclusively for work in rough country. For that, he has to possess stamina and endurance, be merry and active and have a loyal, biddable and amiable temperament, as he must work within a group of other dogs without quarreling.

These are all qualities sought in a good worker: willingness to please the handler, readiness to go into cover and willingness to learn. Some of these talents can be found in every Welshie, but not every Welshie possesses every desirable trait. Some Welshies are bad retrievers, are gun-shy, will not take cover or are unstoppable. If you intend to acquire a Welshie for work, you must select the puppy that shows the most promise for work and that possesses as many qualifications as possible required for work. What you will find in nearly all Welshies is a lot of energy, strong scenting ability and intelligence.

Since there are a dozen times more English Springers and Cockers than Welsh Springers, Welshies are often overlooked by sportsmen and not many compete in field trials, although professional trainers and judges confirm that they are good workers.

French trialer Welsh Fargo's Cherokee Indian Squaw.

Unfortunately, the pool of working stock is too small to create many more dogs that can compete at field trials and thus attract attention and gain popularity. On the other hand, whereas in Cockers and English Springers the breed has been divided into a "working" and a "show" type, in Welsh Springers we fortunately do not see such a split, and the breed is very fortunate in having "show" breeders that work their Welshies as well.

New owners should always be encouraged to start training their puppy. This is not only because the basic training is good for the

This Welshie is holding a typical practice dummy used in the beginning stages of a gundog's retriever training.

"Found it!" Julita Regal Request practices with a different type of dummy; this one resembles a bird.

professional trainer who can give you a couple of lessons. However, do remember that the lessons are to teach the handler, and then it is up to you, the handler, to teach your dog. Nobody can do that for you, and you must be prepared to put a lot of time and effort into the instruction. Rest assured that the results are well worth it!

The basis for every type of training is obedience and that is where you start with your puppy when he is about three months old. By starting with the elementary exercises (like how to pay attention to you, come, sit, etc.), you get to know your puppy and gain his trust and affection. These are simple exercises and can be done in the house or in the yard.

Then you introduce him to retrieving. Use a small object such as a glove, rabbit skin or a

puppy but also because it may enlarge the working-dog gene pool. Among these puppies there might be hidden talents, and the more talent the better. Should your puppy be one of the talented ones and you persevere with training, it will teach you both quite a lot. For you, as owner, training is interesting and useful and gives you a greater understanding of your dog. Moreover, for both of you it is great fun. It will give purpose and pleasure to your daily walks and it will keep you both healthy and in good condition.

You have to start at an early age. Get as much information about training methods as possible and get practical help. If you have no practical knowledge of shooting and no experience with training, you need the advice and help of other people, which is probably best found through your breed club. If there are no training classes available, you can teach your dog yourself from a good manual or you might try to find a

wing of a bird. If you throw the object a few yards ahead of your puppy, he will run to it and pick it up. Call him by his name and encourage him to bring it back to you. Don't be discouraged if your puppy thinks this is a lovely game and runs off with the object! If he does that, move away from him, calling his name. If he runs off again the second time, have him on a light line, so that you can—very lightly—pull him in while calling his name. Always remember to reward him whenever possible. Don't make the lessons too long; from 5 to 20 minutes a day is more than enough to keep it fun for your puppy and for you.

As most of the time is spent correcting mistakes, it is important that you try to think ahead and anticipate what the puppy

will do next so that you avoid mistakes. Once he has acquired a bad habit, you will have to start all over again.

After a couple of months you can teach him to heel and to stay on command. Remember that you achieve more when the puppy makes slow but steady progress than by going too fast and risking constant repetition of the exercise. Remember also to end each lesson with a mastered exercise and praise. Never end with failure.

The next lesson is to encourage him to use his nose. By dragging a bird wing, you can make a trail for him to work out. You can also throw an object into light cover, out of sight, and encourage your Welshie to locate and then to retrieve it. You must be very careful with the puppy when he is teething because picking up the object might be quite painful, and forcing him to pick it up would do irreparable harm to his willingness to retrieve.

Julita Rainspeckle, retrieving the rabbit during a field test.

THE BEST INVESTMENT

Obedience school is as important for you and your dog as grammar school is for your kids, and it's a lot more fun! Don't shun classes thinking that your dog might embarrass you. He might! Instructors don't expect you to know everything, but they'll teach you the correct way to teach your dog so he won't embarrass you again. He'll become a social animal as you learn with other people and dogs. Home training, while effective in teaching your dog the basic commands, excludes these socialization benefits.

TEACHER'S PET

Dogs are individuals, not robots, with many traits basic to their breed. Some, bred to work alone, are independent thinkers; others rely on you to call the shots. If you have enrolled in a training class, your instructor can offer alternative methods of training based on your individual dog's instincts and personality. You may benefit from using a different type of collar or switching to a class with different kinds of dogs.

Right from the start you should prepare your puppy to accept loud banging noises; in fact, this is something the breeder should have done when the puppies were just a couple of weeks old. Start with clapping your hands, banging his food bowl or a bucket, etc. If he shows no fear of such noises, you can introduce him to a starting pistol. Have somebody hold the pup and have the pup sit. You stand away from him while you fire. If he is steady, do not forget to praise him. If that goes well, shorten the distance. He can be introduced to the shotgun later, but he first has to get used to the shot and to sitting beside you with you firing over his head. You can also use a dummy launcher, which will teach him to sit to shot, to mark and to retrieve.

Do not forget to introduce him to water. Start in the summer and find a still pond with shelving sides for his first lessons. He will love the water and learn to plunge in boldly to retrieve.

By the time your puppy is eight or nine months old, knows his basic obedience and has learned to retrieve and use his nose, you can join a more advanced training class. Depending on his natural aptitude you can train for spaniel trials, field trials, hunting tests, tracking and more.

SNIFFER-DOG TRAINING

A new "career" has been discovered for spaniels as sniffer dogs. Sniffer dogs are used to find drugs, explosives and recently also cigarettes hidden in cars, luggage and freight.

Several hundred dogs are being trained each year and for a greater part the training runs on parallel lines with the gundog training, i.e., as far as the dogs' discovering the quarry. The dogs are being trained with dummies that contain a quantity of the target substance.

It seems that the spaniels have taken over this job from the retrievers, because of better scenting abilities and the ability to work for longer periods of time with full concentration.

OTHER ACTIVITIES FOR LIFE
Whether a dog is trained in the structured environment of a class or alone with his owner at home, there are many activities that can bring fun and rewards to both owner and dog once they have mastered basic control.

Teaching the dog to help out around the home, in the yard or on the farm provides great satis-

faction to both dog and owner. In addition, the dog's help makes life a little easier for his owner and raises his stature as a valued companion to his family. It helps give the dog a purpose; it helps to keep his mind occupied and provides an outlet for his energy.

Backpacking is an exciting and healthy activity that the dog can be taught with assistance from his owner. The exercise of walking and climbing is good for man and dog alike, and the bond that they develop together is priceless.

Ch. Saga's Come Fly With Me takes a break from the action to relax at a field event.

OKAY!
This is the signal that tells your dog that he can quit whatever he was doing. Use "Okay" to end a session on a correct response to a command. (Never end on an incorrect response.) Lots of praise follows. People use "Okay" a lot and it has other uses for dogs, too. Your dog is barking. You say, "Okay! Come!" "Okay" signals him to stop the barking activity and "Come" allows him to come to you for a "Good dog."

Julita Roxane completes the retrieve. She is shown here at a field trial in which she had the best performance of the day.

The Welshie is an intelligent and versatile breed who is always ready to lend a paw with household chores.

If you are interested in participating in organized competition with your Welshie, there are other activities apart from obedience and hunting events in which you and your dog can become involved. For example, agility is a popular and enjoyable sport where dogs run through an obstacle course that includes various jumps, tunnels and other exercises to test the dog's speed and coordination. The owners run through the course beside their dogs to give commands and to guide them through the course. Although competitive, the focus is on fun—it's fun to do and fun to watch, as well as great exercise.

Julita Rainspeckle, completing a water retrieve.

HEALTHCARE OF YOUR

WELSH SPRINGER SPANIEL

By Lowell Ackerman DVM, DACVD

HEALTHCARE FOR A LIFETIME

When you own a dog, you become his healthcare advocate over his entire lifespan, as well as being the one to shoulder the financial burden of such care. Accordingly, it is worthwhile to focus on prevention rather than treatment, as you and your pet will both be happier.

Of course, the best place to have begun your program of preventive healthcare is with the initial purchase or adoption of your dog. You certainly should have done adequate research into the Welsh Springer Spaniel and have selected your puppy carefully rather than buying on impulse. Health issues aside, a large number of pet abandonment and relinquishment cases arise from a mismatch between pet needs and owner expectations. This is entirely preventable with appropriate planning and finding a good breeder.

Regarding healthcare issues specifically, it is very difficult to make blanket statements about where to acquire a problem-free pet, but, again, a reputable breeder is your best bet. In an ideal situation you have the opportunity to

see both parents, get references from other owners of the breeder's pups and see genetic-testing documentation for several generations of the litter's ancestors. At the very least, you must thoroughly investigate the Welsh Springer Spaniel and the problems inherent in the breed, as well as the genetic testing available to screen for those problems. Genetic testing offers some important benefits, but testing is available for only a few disorders in a relatively small number of breeds and is not available for some of the most common genetic diseases, such as hip dysplasia, cataracts, epilepsy, cardiomyopathy, etc. This area of research is indeed exciting and increasingly important, and advances will continue to be made each year.

We've also discussed that evaluating the behavioral nature of your Welsh Springer Spaniel and that of his immediate family members is an important part of the selection process that cannot be underestimated or overemphasized. It is sometimes difficult to evaluate temperament in puppies because certain behavioral tendencies, such as some forms of aggression, may not be immedi-

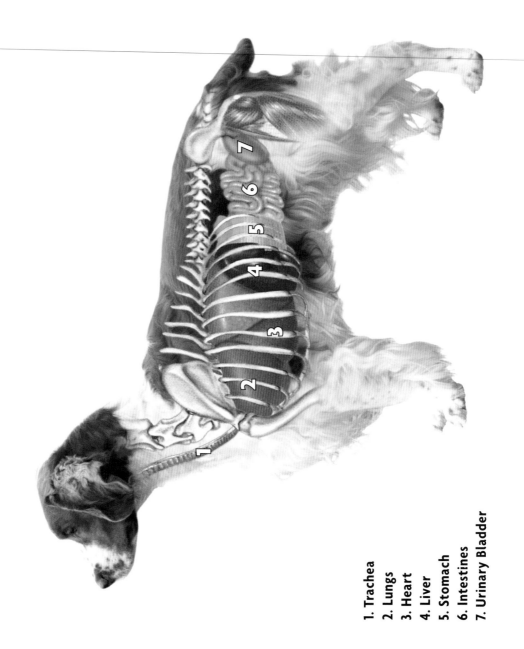

1. Trachea
2. Lungs
3. Heart
4. Liver
5. Stomach
6. Intestines
7. Urinary Bladder

INTERNAL ORGANS OF THE WELSH SPRINGER SPANIEL

ately evident. More dogs are euthanized each year for behavioral reasons than for all medical conditions combined, so it is critical to take temperament issues seriously. Start with a well-balanced, friendly companion and put the time and effort into proper socialization, and you will both be rewarded with a valued relationship for the life of the dog.

Assuming that you have started off with a pup from healthy, sound stock, you then become responsible for helping your veterinarian keep your pet healthy. Some crucial things happen before you even bring your puppy home. Parasite control typically begins at two weeks of age, and vaccinations typically begin at six to eight weeks of age. A pre-pubertal evaluation is typically scheduled for about six months of age. At this time, a dental evaluation is done (since the adult teeth are now in), heartworm prevention is started and neutering or spaying is most commonly done.

It is critical to commence regular dental care at home if you have not already done so. It may not sound very important, but most dogs have active periodontal disease by four years of age if they don't have their teeth cleaned regularly at home, not just at their veterinary exams. Dental problems lead to more than just bad "doggy breath." Gum disease can

have very serious medical consequences. If you start brushing your dog's teeth and using antiseptic rinses from a young age, your dog will be accustomed to it and will not resist. The results will be healthy dentition, which your pet will need to enjoy a long, healthy life.

Even individual dogs within each breed have different healthcare requirements, so work with your veterinarian to determine what will be needed and what your role should be. This doctor-client relationship is important. You must make sure that you see your veterinarian at least annually, even if no vaccines are due, because this is the best opportunity to coordinate healthcare activities and to make sure that no medical issues creep by unaddressed.

At around eight years old or as determined by the vet, your Welshie will be considered a "senior" and will require some

Sammi is happy, healthy and enjoying herself in the great outdoors.

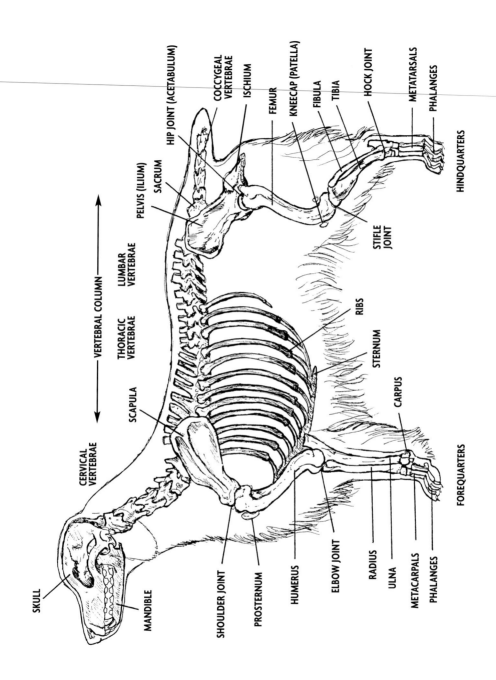

CERVICAL VERTEBRAE

VERTEBRAL COLUMN

THORACIC VERTEBRAE

LUMBAR VERTEBRAE

PELVIS (ILIUM)

SACRUM

HIP JOINT (ACETABULUM)

COCCYGEAL VERTEBRAE

ISCHIUM

FEMUR

KNEECAP (PATELLA)

FIBULA

TIBIA

HOCK JOINT

METATARSALS

PHALANGES

HINDQUARTERS

STIFLE JOINT

RIBS

STERNUM

SCAPULA

CARPUS

SKULL

MANDIBLE

SHOULDER JOINT

PROSTERNUM

HUMERUS

ELBOW JOINT

RADIUS

ULNA

METACARPALS

PHALANGES

FOREQUARTERS

SKELETAL STRUCTURE OF THE WELSH SPRINGER SPANIEL

special care. In general, if you've been taking great care of your canine companion throughout his formative and adult years, the transition to senior status should be a smooth one. Age is not a disease, and as long as everything is functioning as it should, there is no reason why most of late adulthood should not be rewarding for both you and your pet. This is especially true if you have tended to the details, such as regular veterinary visits, proper dental care, excellent nutrition and management of bone and joint issues.

At this stage in your Welsh Springer Spaniel's life, your veterinarian may want to schedule visits twice yearly, instead of once, to run some laboratory screenings, electrocardiograms and the like, and to change the diet to something more digestible. Catching problems early is the best way to manage them effectively. Treating the early stages of heart disease is so much easier than trying to intervene when there is more significant damage to the heart muscle. Similarly, managing the beginning of kidney problems is fairly routine if there is no significant kidney damage. Other problems, like cognitive dysfunction (similar to senility and Alzheimer's disease), cancer, diabetes and arthritis, are more common in older dogs, but all can be treated to help the dog live as

many happy, comfortable years as possible. Just as in people, medical management is more effective (and less expensive) when you catch things early.

SELECTING A VETERINARIAN
There is probably no more important decision that you will make regarding your pet's healthcare than the selection of his doctor. Your pet's veterinarian will be a pediatrician, family-practice physician and gerontologist, depending on the dog's life stage, and will be the individual who makes recommendations regarding issues such as when specialists need to be consulted, when diagnostic testing and/or therapeutic intervention is needed and when you will need to seek outside emergency and critical-care services. Your vet will act as your advocate and liaison

Two handsome and sprightly seniors: on the left, Ch. Killagay's Sherlock Holmes ("Kirby"), age ten; on the right, Ch. Penri Tomas O'Killagay ("Thomas"), age nine.

throughout these processes. Everyone has his own idea about what to look for in a vet, an individual who will play a big role in his dog's (and, of course, his own) life for many years to come. For some, it is the compassionate caregiver with whom they hope to develop a professional relationship to span the lives of their dogs and even their future pets. For others, they are seeking a clinician who can deliver state-of-the-art healthcare. Still others need a veterinary facility that can to accommodate their schedules; these people may not much mind that their dogs might see different veterinarians on each visit. Just as we have different reasons for selecting our own healthcare professionals, we should not expect that there is a one-size-fits-all recommendation for selecting a veterinarian and veterinary practice. The best advice is to be honest in your assessment of what you expect from a veterinary practice and to conscientiously research the options in your area. You will quickly appreciate that not all veterinary practices are the same, and you will be happiest with one that truly meets your needs.

There is another point to be considered in the selection of veterinary services. Not that long ago, a single veterinarian would attempt to manage all medical and surgical issues as they arose. That was often problematic, because it was just impossible for general veterinary practitioners to be experts in every species, every breed, every field and every ailment. However, just as in the human healthcare fields, specialization has allowed general practitioners to concentrate on primary healthcare delivery, especially wellness and preventive care, and to utilize a network of specialists to assist in the management of conditions that require specific expertise and experience. Thus there are now many types of veterinary specialists, including dermatologists, cardiologists, ophthalmologists, surgeons, internists, oncologists, neurologists, behaviorists, criticalists and others to help primary-care veterinarians deal with complicated medical challenges. In most cases, specialists see cases referred by primary-care veterinarians, make diagnoses and set up management plans. From there, the animals' ongoing care is returned to their primary-care veterinarians. This important team approach to your pet's medical-care needs has provided opportunities for an unparalleled level of care to be delivered.

With all of the opportunities for your Welsh Springer Spaniel to receive high-quality veterinary medical care, there is another topic that needs to be addressed at the same time—cost. It's been said that you can have excellent healthcare

cocoons, they orient towards light; thus when an animal passes between a flea and the light source, casting a shadow, the flea pounces and starts to feed. If the animal turns out to be a dog or cat, the reproductive cycle continues. If the flea lands on another type of animal, including a person, the flea will bite but will then look for a more appropriate host. An emerging adult flea can survive without feeding for up to 12 months but, once it tastes blood, it can survive off its host for only 3 to 4 days.

It was once thought that fleas spend most of their lives in the environment, but we now know that fleas won't willingly jump off a dog unless leaping to another dog or when physically removed by brushing, bathing or other manipulation. Flea eggs, on the other hand, are shiny and smooth, and they roll off the animal and into the environment. The eggs, larvae and pupae then exist in the environment, but once the adult finds a susceptible animal, it's home sweet home until the flea is forced to seek refuge elsewhere.

Since adult fleas live on the animal and immature forms survive in the environment, a successful treatment plan must address all stages of the flea life cycle. There are now several safe and effective flea-control products that can be applied on a monthly basis. These include fipronil, imidacloprid, selamectin and

> ### FLEA PREVENTION FOR YOUR DOG
> - Discuss with your veterinarian the safest product to protect your dog, likely in the form of a monthly tablet or a liquid preparation placed on the back of the dog's neck.
> - For dogs suffering from flea-bite dermatitis, a shampoo or topical insecticide treatment is required.
> - Your lawn and property should be sprayed with an insecticide designed to kill fleas and ticks that lurk outdoors.
> - Using a flea comb, check the dog's coat regularly for any signs of parasites.
> - Practice good housekeeping. Vacuum floors, carpets and furniture regularly, especially in the areas that the dog frequents, and wash the dog's bedding weekly.
> - Follow up house-cleaning with carpet shampoos and sprays to rid the house of fleas at all stages of development. Insect growth regulators are the safest option.

permethrin (found in several formulations). Most of these products have significant flea-killing rates within 24 hours. Nitenpyram, an oral tablet, can even quickly kill fleas in a couple of hours and can be used once a day. However, none of them will control the immature forms in the environment. To accomplish this, there are a variety of insect growth regulators that can

THE FLEA'S LIFE CYCLE

What came first, the flea or the egg? This age-old mystery is more difficult to comprehend than the

actual cycle of the flea. Fleas usually live only about four months. A female can lay 2,000 eggs in her lifetime.

Photo by Carolina Biological Supply Co.

Egg

After ten days of rolling around your carpet or under your furniture, the eggs hatch into larvae, which feed on various and sundry debris. In days or

Larva

Photo by Carolina Biological Supply Co.

months, depending on the climate, the larvae spin cocoons and develop into the pupal or nymph stage, which quickly develop into fleas.

Pupa

These immature fleas must locate a host within 10 to 14 days or they will die. Only about 1% of the flea population exist as adult fleas, while the other 99% exist as eggs, larvae or pupae.

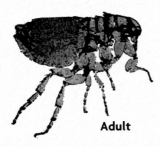

Adult

KILL FLEAS THE NATURAL WAY

If you choose not to go the route of conventional medication, there are some natural ways to ward off fleas:

• Dust your dog with a natural flea powder, composed of such herbal goodies as rosemary, wormwood, pennyroyal, citronella, rue, tobacco powder and eucalyptus.

• Apply diatomaceous earth, the fossilized remains of single-cell algae, to your carpets, furniture and pet's bedding. Even though it's not good for dogs, it's even worse for fleas, which will dry up swiftly and die.

• Brush your dog frequently, give him adequate exercise and let him fast occasionally. All of these activities strengthen the dog's immune system and make him more resistant to disease and parasites.

• Bathe your dog with a capful of pennyroyal or eucalyptus oil.

• Feed a natural diet, free of additives and preservatives. Add some fresh garlic and brewer's yeast to the dog's morning portion, as these items have flea-repelling properties.

be sprayed into the environment (e.g., pyriproxyfen, methoprene, fenoxycarb) as well as insect development inhibitors such as lufenuron that can be administered. These compounds have no effect on adult fleas, but they stop immature forms from developing into

adults. In years gone by, we relied heavily on toxic insecticides (such as organophosphates, organochlorines and carbamates) to manage the flea problem, but today's options are not only much safer to use on our pets but also safer for the environment.

TICKS

Ticks are members of the spider class (arachnids) and are blood-sucking parasites capable of transmitting a variety of diseases, including Lyme disease, ehrlichiosis, babesiosis and Rocky Mountain spotted fever. It's easy to see ticks on your own skin, but it is more of a challenge when your furry companion is affected. Whenever you happen to be planning a stroll in a tick-infested area (especially forests, grassy or wooded areas or parks) be prepared to do a thorough inspection of your dog afterward to search for ticks. Ticks can be tricky, so make sure you spend time looking in the ears, between the toes and everywhere else where a tick might hide. Ticks need to be attached for 24–72 hours before they transmit most of the diseases that they carry, so you do have a window of opportunity for some preventive intervention.

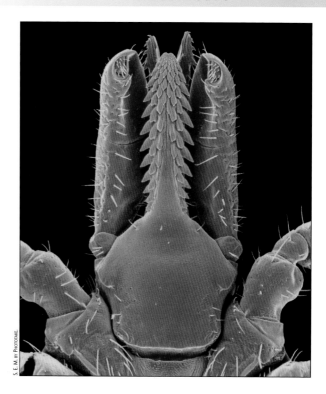

S.E.M. BY PHOTOTAKE.

A scanning electron micrograph of the head of a female deer tick, *Ixodes dammini,* a parasitic tick that carries Lyme disease.

A TICKING BOMB

There is nothing good about a tick's harpooning his nose into your dog's skin. Among the diseases caused by ticks are Rocky Mountain spotted fever, canine ehrlichiosis, canine babesiosis, canine hepatozoonosis and Lyme disease. If a dog is allergic to the saliva of a female wood tick, he can develop tick paralysis.

Female ticks live to eat and breed. They can lay between 4,000 and 5,000 eggs and they die soon after. Males, on the other hand, live only to mate with the females and continue the process as long as they are able. Most ticks live on multiple hosts before parasitizing dogs. The immature forms typically reside on grass and shrubs, waiting for susceptible animals to walk by. The larvae and nymph stages typically feed on wildlife.

If only a few ticks are present on a dog, they can be plucked out, but it is important to remove the entire head and mouthparts,

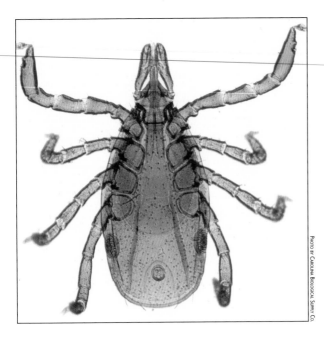

Deer tick,
Ixodes dammini.

Photo by Carolina Biological Supply Co.

of in a container of alcohol or household bleach.

Some of the newer flea products, specifically those with fipronil, selamectin and permethrin, have effect against some, but not all, species of tick. Flea collars containing appropriate pesticides (e.g., propoxur, chlorfenvinphos) can aid in tick control. In most areas, such collars should be placed on animals in March, at the beginning of the tick season, and changed regularly. Leaving the collar on when the pesticide level is waning invites the development of resistance. Amitraz collars are also good for tick control, and the active ingredient does not interfere with other flea-control products. The ingredient helps prevent the attachment of ticks to the skin and will cause those ticks already on the skin to detach themselves.

which may be deeply embedded in the skin. This is best accomplished with forceps designed especially for this purpose; fingers can be used but should be protected with rubber gloves, plastic wrap or at least a paper towel. The tick should be grasped as closely as possible to the animal's skin and should be pulled upward with steady, even pressure. Do not squeeze, crush or puncture the body of the tick or you risk exposure to any disease carried by that tick. Once the ticks have been removed, the sites of attachment should be disinfected. Your hands should then be washed with soap and water to further minimize risk of contagion. The tick should be disposed

---

TICK CONTROL

Removal of underbrush and leaf litter and the thinning of trees in areas where tick control is desired are recommended. These actions remove the cover and food sources for small animals that serve as hosts for ticks. With continued mowing of grasses in these areas, the probability of ticks' surviving is further reduced. A variety of insecticide ingredients (e.g., resmethrin, carbaryl, permethrin, chlorpyrifos, dioxathion and allethrin) are registered for tick control around the home.

MITES

Mites are tiny arachnid parasites that parasitize the skin of dogs. Skin diseases caused by mites are referred to as "mange," and there are many different forms seen in dogs. These forms are very different from one another, each one warranting an individual description.

Sarcoptic mange, or scabies, is one of the itchiest conditions that affects dogs. The microscopic *Sarcoptes* mites burrow into the superficial layers of the skin and can drive dogs crazy with itchiness. They are also communicable to people, although they can't complete their reproductive cycle on people. In addition to being tiny, the mites also are often difficult to find when trying to make a diagnosis. Skin scrapings from multiple areas are examined microscopically but, even then, sometimes the mites cannot be found.

Fortunately, scabies is relatively easy to treat, and there are a variety of products that will successfully kill the mites. Since the mites can't live in the environment for very long without feeding, a complete cure is usually possible within four to eight weeks.

Cheyletiellosis is caused by a relatively large mite, which sometimes can be seen even without a microscope. Often referred to as "walking dandruff," this also causes itching, but not usually as profound as with scabies. While *Cheyletiella*

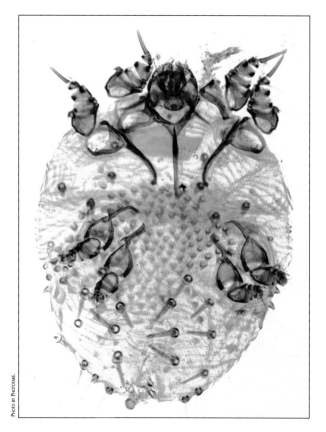

PHOTO BY PHOTOTAKE.

mites can survive somewhat longer in the environment than scabies mites, they too are relatively easy to treat, being responsive to not only the medications used to treat scabies but also often to flea-control products.

Otodectes cynotis is the canine ear mite and is one of the more common causes of mange, especially in young dogs in shelters or pet stores. That's because the mites are typically present in large numbers and are quickly spread to nearby animals. The mites rarely do

**Sarcoptes scabiei,
commonly known
as the "itch mite."**

Micrograph of a dog louse, *Heterodoxus spiniger*. Female lice attach their eggs to the hairs of the dog. As the eggs hatch, the larval lice bite and feed on the blood. Lice can also feed on dead skin and hair. This feeding activity can cause hair loss and skin problems.

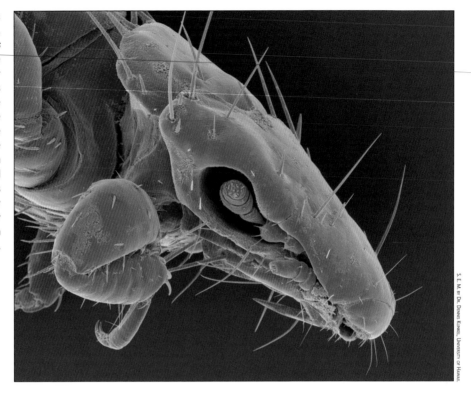

S. E. M. by Dr. Dennis Kunkel, University of Hawaii.

much harm but can be difficult to eradicate if the treatment regimen is not comprehensive. While many try to treat the condition with ear drops only, this is the most common cause of treatment failure. Ear drops cause the mites to simply move out of the ears and as far away as possible (usually to the base of the tail) until the insecticide levels in the ears drop to an acceptable level—then it's back to business as usual! The successful treatment of ear mites requires treating all animals in the household with a systemic insecticide, such as selamectin, or a combination of miticidal ear drops

combined with whole-body flea-control preparations.

Demodicosis, sometimes referred to as red mange, can be one of the most difficult forms of mange to treat. Part of the problem has to do with the fact that the mites live in the hair follicles and they are relatively well shielded from topical and systemic products. The main issue, however, is that demodectic mange typically results only when there is some underlying process interfering with the dog's immune system.

Since *Demodex* mites are normal residents of the skin of

mammals, including humans, there is usually a mite population explosion only when the immune system fails to keep the number of mites in check. In young animals, the immune deficit may be transient or may reflect an actual inherited immune problem. In older animals, demodicosis is usually seen only when there is another disease hampering the immune system, such as diabetes, cancer, thyroid problems or the use of immune-suppressing drugs. Accordingly, treatment involves not only trying to kill the mange mites but also discerning what is interfering with immune function and correcting it if possible.

Chiggers represent several different species of mite that don't parasitize dogs specifically, but do latch on to passersby and can cause irritation. The problem is most prevalent in wooded areas in the late summer and fall. Treatment is not difficult, as the mites do not complete their life cycle on dogs and are susceptible to a variety of miticidal products.

MOSQUITOES

Mosquitoes have long been known to transmit a variety of diseases to people, as well as just being biting pests during warm weather. They also pose a real risk to pets. Not only do they carry deadly heartworms but recently there also has been much concern over their involvement with West Nile virus. While we can avoid heartworm with the use of preventive medications, there are no such preventives for West Nile virus. The only method of prevention in endemic areas is active mosquito control. Fortunately, most dogs that have been exposed to the virus only developed flu-like symptoms and, to date, there have not been the large number of reported deaths in canines as seen in some other species.

Illustration of *Demodex folliculoram*.

ILLUSTRATION BY PHOTOTAKE.

MOSQUITO REPELLENT

Low concentrations of DEET (less than 10%), found in many human mosquito repellents, have been safely used on dogs but, in these concentrations, probably give only about two hours of protection. DEET may be safe in these small concentrations, but since it is not licensed for use on dogs, there is no research proving its safety for dogs. Products containing permethrin give the longest-lasting protection, perhaps two to four weeks. As DEET is not licensed for use on dogs, and both DEET and permethrin can be quite toxic to cats, appropriate care should be exercised. Other products, such as those containing oil of citronella, also have some mosquito-repellent activity, but typically have a relatively short duration of action.

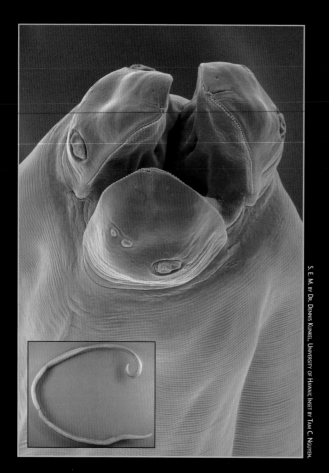

S. E. M. BY DR. DENNIS KUNKEL, UNIVERSITY OF HAWAII. INSET BY TAM C. NGUYEN.

The ascarid roundworm *Toxocara canis,* showing the mouth with three lips. INSET: Photomicrograph of the roundworm *Ascaris lumbricoides.*

INTERNAL PARASITES: WORMS

ASCARIDS

Ascarids are intestinal roundworms that rarely cause severe disease in dogs. Nonetheless, they are of major public health significance because they can be transferred to people. Sadly, it is children who are most commonly affected by the parasite, probably from inadvertently ingesting ascarid-contaminated soil. In fact, many yards and children's sandboxes contain appreciable numbers of ascarid eggs. So, while ascarids don't bite dogs or latch onto their intestines to suck blood, they do cause some nasty medical conditions in children and are best eradicated from our furry friends. Because pups can start passing ascarid eggs by three weeks of age, most parasite-control programs begin at two weeks of age and are repeated every two weeks until pups are eight weeks old. It is important to

S. E. M. BY DR. DENNIS KUNKEL, UNIVERSITY OF HAWAII.

realize that bitches can pass ascarids to their pups even if they test negative prior to whelping. Accordingly, bitches are best treated at the same time as the pups.

HOOKWORMS

Unlike ascarids, hookworms do latch onto a dog's intestinal tract and can cause significant loss of blood and protein. Similar to ascarids, hookworms can be transmitted to humans, where they cause a condition known as cutaneous larval migrans. Dogs can become infected either by consuming the infective larvae or by the larvae's penetrating the skin directly. People most often get infected when they are lying on the ground (such as on a beach) and the larvae penetrate the skin. Yes, the larvae can penetrate through a beach blanket. Hookworms are typically susceptible to the same medications used to treat ascarids.

The hookworm *Ancylostoma caninum* infests the intestines of dogs. INSET: Note the row of hooks at the posterior end, used to anchor the worm to the intestinal wall.

WHIPWORMS

Whipworms latch onto the lower aspects of the dog's colon and can cause cramping and diarrhea. Eggs do not start to appear in the dog's feces until about three months after the dog was infected. This worm has a peculiar life cycle, which makes it more difficult to control than ascarids or hookworms. The good thing is that whipworms rarely are transferred to people.

Some of the medications used to treat ascarids and hookworms are also effective against whipworms, but, in general, a separate treatment protocol is needed. Since most of the medications are effective against the adults but not the eggs or larvae, treatment is typically repeated in three weeks, and then often in three

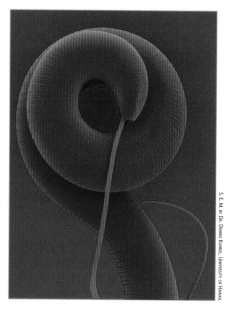

Adult whipworm, *Trichuris* sp., an intestinal parasite.

S. E. M. BY DR. DENNIS KUNKEL, UNIVERSITY OF HAWAII.

WORM-CONTROL GUIDELINES

• Practice sanitary habits with your dog and home.
• Clean up after your dog and don't let him sniff or eat other dogs' droppings.
• Control insects and fleas in the dog's environment. Fleas, lice, cockroaches, beetles, mice and rats can act as hosts for various worms.
• Prevent dogs from eating uncooked meat, raw poultry and dead animals.
• Keep dogs and children from playing in sand and soil.
• Kennel dogs on cement or gravel; avoid dirt runs.
• Administer heartworm preventives regularly.
• Have your vet examine your dog's stools at your annual visits.
• Select a boarding kennel carefully so as to avoid contamination from other dogs or an unsanitary environment.
• Prevent dogs from roaming. Obey local leash laws.

months as well. Unfortunately, since dogs don't develop resistance to whipworms, it is difficult to prevent them from getting reinfected if they visit soil contaminated with whipworm eggs.

TAPEWORMS

There are many different species of tapeworm that affect dogs, but *Dipylidium caninum* is probably the most common and is spread by fleas. Flea larvae feed on organic debris and tapeworm eggs in the environment and, when a dog chews at himself and manages to ingest fleas, he might get a dose of tapeworm at the same time. The tapeworm then develops further in the intestine of the dog.

The tapeworm itself, which is a parasitic flatworm that latches onto the intestinal wall, is composed of numerous segments. When the segments break off into the intestine (as proglottids), they may accumulate around the rectum, like grains of rice. While this tapeworm is disgusting in its behavior, it is not directly communicable to humans (although humans can also get infected by swallowing fleas).

A much more dangerous tapeworm is *Echinococcus multilocularis*, which is typically found in foxes, coyotes and wolves. The eggs are passed in the feces and infect rodents, and, when dogs eat the rodents, the dogs can be infected by thousands of adult tapeworms. While the parasites don't cause many problems in dogs, this is considered the most lethal worm infection that people can get. Take appropriate precautions if you live in an area in which these tapeworms are found. Do not use mulch that may contain feces of dogs, cats or wildlife, and discourage your pets from hunting wildlife. Treat these tapeworm infections aggressively in pets, because if humans get infected, approximately half die.

HEARTWORMS

Heartworm disease is caused by the parasite *Dirofilaria immitis* and is seen in dogs around the world. A member of the roundworm group, it is spread between dogs by the bite of an infected mosquito. The mosquito injects infective larvae into the dog's skin with its bite, and these larvae develop under the skin for a period of time before making their way to the heart. There they develop into adults, which grow and create blockages of the heart, lungs and major blood vessels there. They also start producing offspring (microfilariae),

A dog tapeworm proglottid (body segment).

The dog tapeworm *Taenia pisiformis*.

S. E. M. BY DR. DENNIS KUNKEL, UNIVERSITY OF HAWAII.

A Look at Internal Parasites

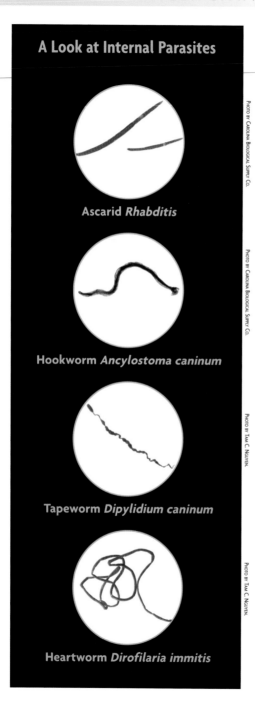

Ascarid *Rhabditis*

Hookworm *Ancylostoma caninum*

Tapeworm *Dipylidium caninum*

Heartworm *Dirofilaria immitis*

PHOTO BY CAROLINA BIOLOGICAL SUPPLY CO.

PHOTO BY CAROLINA BIOLOGICAL SUPPLY CO.

PHOTO BY TAM C. NGUYEN.

PHOTO BY TAM C. NGUYEN.

and these microfilariae circulate in the bloodstream, waiting to hitch a ride when the next mosquito bites. Once in the mosquito, the microfilariae develop into infective larvae and the entire process is repeated.

When dogs get infected with heartworm, over time they tend to develop symptoms associated with heart disease, such as coughing, exercise intolerance and potentially many other manifestations. Diagnosis is confirmed by either seeing the microfilariae themselves in blood samples or using immunologic tests (antigen testing) to identify the presence of adult heartworms. Since antigen tests measure the presence of adult heartworms and microfilarial tests measure offspring produced by adults, neither are positive until six to seven months after the initial infection. However, the beginning of damage can occur by fifth-stage larvae as early as three months after infection. Thus it is possible for dogs to be harboring problem-causing larvae for up to three months before either type of test would identify an infection.

The good news is that there are great protocols available for preventing heartworm in dogs. Testing is critical in the process, and it is important to understand the benefits as well as the limitations of such testing. All dogs six months of age or older that have not been on continuous heartworm-preventive medication should be

same breed to decide which they think is the better specimen; in the Group and Best in Show ring, however, it is very difficult to compare one breed to another, like apples to oranges. Thus the dog's conformation to the breed standard—not to mention advertising dollars and good handling— is essential to success in conformation shows. The dog described in the standard (the standard for each AKC breed is written and approved by the breed's national parent club and then submitted to the AKC for approval) is the perfect dog of that breed, and

breeders keep their eye on the standard when they choose which dogs to breed, hoping to get closer and closer to the ideal with each litter.

Ch. Trystyn's Hula Popper, owned by Sandra Holmes and Meghen Bassel, has multiple Group placements and is one of the few bitches to win Best of Breed at the American Spaniel Club.

Another good first step for the novice is to join a dog club. You will be astonished by the many and different kinds of dog clubs in the country, with about 5,000 clubs holding events every year. Most clubs require that prospective new members present two letters of recommendation from existing members. Perhaps you've made some friends visiting a show held by a particular club and you would like to join that club. Dog clubs may specialize in a single breed, like a local or regional Welsh Springer Spaniel club, or in a specific pursuit, such as obedience, tracking or hunting tests. There are all-breed clubs for all dog enthusiasts; they sponsor special training days, seminars on topics like grooming or handling or lectures on breeding or canine

Shelley Traylor in the ring with Ch. Rolyart's Still the One WD, CGC, one of the breed's big winners and a dog who shows us that competition isn't all work and no fun.

Best of Breed for Ch. Penri Tomas O'Killagay, ("Thomas"), owned by Connie Christie, Harry Holmes and Beth Holmes (pictured). Thomas was owner/handled for most of his impressive show career, which includes two American Spaniel Club Best of Breed wins, two Westminster Awards of Merit and two Group placements.

genetics. There are also clubs that specialize in certain types of dogs, like herding dogs, hunting dogs, companion dogs, etc.

A parent club is the national organization, sanctioned by the AKC, which promotes and safe-guards its breed in the country. The Welsh Springer Spaniel Club of America was formed in 1961 and can be contacted on the Internet at www.wssca.com. The parent club holds an annual national specialty show, usually in a different city each year, in which many of the country's top dogs, handlers and breeders gather to compete. At a specialty show, only members of a single breed are invited to participate. There are also group specialties, in which all members of a group are invited. For more information about dog clubs in your area, contact the AKC at www.akc.org

on the Internet or write them at 5580 Centerview Drive, Raleigh, NC 27606.

OTHER TYPES OF COMPETITION
In addition to conformation shows, the AKC holds a variety of other competitive events. Obedience trials, agility trials and tracking tests are open to all breeds, while hunting tests, field trials, lure coursing, herding tests and trials, earthdog tests and coonhound events are limited to specific breeds or groups of breeds. The Junior Showmanship Program is offered to aspiring

FIVE CLASSES AT SHOWS
At most AKC all-breed shows, there are six regular classes offered: Puppy, 12–18 Months, Novice, Bred-by-Exhibitor, American-bred and Open. The Puppy Class is usually divided as 6 to 9 months of age and 9 to 12 months of age. When deciding in which class to enter your dog, whether male or female, you must carefully check the show schedule to make sure that you have selected the right class. Depending on the age of the dog, previous first-place wins and the sex of the dog, you must make the best choice. It is possible to enter a one-year-old dog who has not won sufficient first places in any of the non-Puppy Classes, though the competition is more intense the further you progress from the Puppy Class.

AMERICA'S ALTERNATIVE: THE UNITED KENNEL CLUB

The United Kennel Club (UKC) defines itself as follows: "With 300,000 registrations annually, the United Kennel Club is the world's largest performance dog registry and second oldest all-breed registry in the United States. Founded in 1898, the UKC has supported the 'Total Dog' philosophy through its events and programs for over a century. As a departure from registries that place emphasis on a dog's looks, UKC events are designed for dogs that look and perform equally well." Professional handlers are not permitted in UKC shows, and the club goes on to state, "At UKC dog shows, the emphasis is on the dog, not the show."

True to its aim of promoting the "Total Dog," the UKC hosts conformation events as well as a multitude of performance events, including obedience trials; agility trials; field trials, water races, nite hunts and bench shows for coonhound breeds; hunting tests for retrieving breeds; Beagle events, including hunts and bench shows; squirrel and coon events and bench shows for Cur and Feist; weight pulling and more. There is a junior handling program to encourage the next generation of up-and-coming responsible owners and participants in the dog sport.

For more information, visit the UKC online at www.ukcdogs.com.

young handlers and their dogs, and the Canine Good Citizen® Program is an all-around good-behavior test open to all dogs, pure-bred and mixed.

OBEDIENCE TRIALS

Mrs. Helen Whitehouse Walker, a Standard Poodle fancier, can be credited with introducing obedience trials to the United States. In the 1930s she designed a series of exercises based on those of the Associated Sheep, Police, Army Dog Society of Great Britain. These exercises were intended to evaluate the working relationship between dog and owner. Since those early days of the sport in the US, obedience trials have grown more and more popular, and now more than 2,000 trials each year attract over 100,000 dogs and their owners.

Pictured at the 1991 WSSCA national specialty are (from left to right): Mr. John Phillips, a judge from the UK; Mrs. Carol Krohn with Ch. Tydaky's Wildfire; Mrs. Susan Riese, president of the WSSCA; and Mrs. Ria Hörter, breeder from the Netherlands. Mrs. Hörter was the breeder of Dutch and German Ch. Valentijn van Snellestein, a very influential import into the US and a top producer.

Ch. Holly House Sweet William, owned by Anne Legare, was the 2005 Founder's Cup winner, which is an award presented to the Welsh Springer who defeats the most of his breed in conformation for the year.

level is the Utility Class, in which dogs compete for the Utility Dog (UD) title. Classes at each level are further divided into "A" and "B," with "A" for beginners and "B" for those with more experience. In order to win a title at a given level, a dog must earn three "legs." A "leg" is accomplished when a dog scores 170 or higher (200 is a perfect score). Available points for each exercise range between 20 and 40.

Once he's earned the UD title, a dog can go on to win the prestigious title of Utility Dog Excellent (UDX) by winning "legs" in ten shows. Additionally, Utility Dogs who win "legs" in Open B and Utility B earn points toward the lofty title of Obedience Trial Champion (OTCh.). Established in 1977 by the AKC, this title requires a dog to earn 100 points as well as 3 first places in a combination of Open B and Utility B classes under 3 different judges. The "brass ring" of obedience competition is the AKC's National Obedience Invitational. This is an exclusive competition for only the cream of the obedience crop. In order to qualify for the invitational, a dog must be ranked in either the top 25 all-breeds in obedience or in the top 3 for his breed in obedience. The title at stake here is that of National Obedience Champion (NOC).

Any dog registered with the AKC, regardless of neutering or other disqualifications that would preclude entry in conformation competition, can participate in obedience trials.

There are three levels of difficulty in obedience competition. The first (and easiest) level is the Novice Class, in which dogs can earn the Companion Dog (CD) title. The intermediate level is the Open Class, in which the Companion Dog Excellent (CDX) title is awarded. The advanced

TRACKING

Tracking tests are exciting ways to test your Welsh Springer Spaniel's instinctive scenting ability on a competitive level. All dogs have a nose, and all breeds are welcome in tracking tests. The first AKC-licensed tracking test took place in 1937 as part of the Utility level at an obedience trial, and thus competitive tracking was officially begun. The first title, Tracking Dog (TD), was offered in 1947, ten years after the first official tracking test. It was not until 1980 that the AKC added the title Tracking Dog Excellent (TDX), which was followed by the title Variable Surface Tracking (VST) in 1995. Champion Tracker (CT) is awarded to a dog who has earned all three of those titles.

The TD level is the first and most basic level in tracking, progressing in difficulty to the TDX and then the VST. A dog must follow a track laid by a human 30 to 120 minutes prior in order to earn the TD title. The track is about 500 yards long and contains up to 5 directional changes. At the next level, the TDX, the dog must follow a 3- to 5-hour-old track over a course that is up to 1,000 yards long and has up to 7 directional changes. In the most difficult level, the VST, the track is up to 5 hours old and located in an urban setting.

Advanced/Excellent. The dog and handler go through a series of exercises designed by the judge and are timed. Signs are set up around the ring to indicate which exercise (or combination of exercises) is required. Working closely around the course, the team heels from one sign to the next, performing the various exercises. There are 50 exercises to choose from, varying in complexity and difficulty.

The handlers are encouraged to talk to their dogs as they work through the course. The judge evaluates each team on how well it executes one continuous performance over the whole course. The team works on its own as soon as the judge gives the order to begin. Handlers develop their own style in working with their dogs, using a combination of body language and hand signals as well as verbal commands. Faster and more accurate performances are desirable, though each team must work at its own pace.

The dogs love this sport and it shows by their animation and energy. Many of the dogs who participate in obedience or agility also do well in rally. While most of the first rally titles have gone to seasoned obedience dogs, it's encouraging that some newcomers have also earned awards. Rally is a good way for a beginner to start out in obedience. We hope that it will become a stepping stone to the obedience world and we will see many more dogs and owners coming into the ring.

INDEX

My Welsh Springer Spaniel

PUT YOUR PUPPY'S FIRST PICTURE HERE

Dog's Name _____

Date _____ Photographer _____